HOW YOU CAN MA[...]

$25,000

A YEAR WITH YOUR
CAMERA
NO MATTER WHERE YOU LIVE

HOW YOU CAN MAKE

$25,000

A YEAR
WITH YOUR
CAMERA

NO MATTER WHERE YOU LIVE

LARRY CRIBB

Writer's
Digest
Books

Cincinnati, Ohio

First printing October, 1981
Second printing April, 1982

All photographs by the author.

Library of Congress Cataloging in Publication Data

Cribb, Larry, 1934-
    How to make $25,000 a year with your camera.

    Includes index.
    1. Photography, Freelance. I. Title.
TR690.2.C74   1981   770'.68   81-11589
ISBN 0-89879-059-X   AACR2
ISBN 0-89879-060-3 (pbk.)

Book design by Colophon.

To my family,
and to Jack and Mary McGrail,
who shared their knowledge and their friendship

Introduction

I have tried to pack thirty-one years of photographic experience into this book. The whole point of my writing has been to provide the freelance photographer, or the would-be freelancer, with ideas and suggestions for making money with his or her camera.

I have worked at every job discussed in these pages—from weekly newspapers to garden clubs to weddings—and have proven that they can work. Nothing has been included just because it makes for good reading.

This is an *idea* book. If you gain one client—if you get just one job assignment—you'll have recouped your investment in this volume.

If you follow the advice contained herein, I guarantee that you'll be able to make a good income from your photography—provided you're a good photographer. This is a book for *freelance*, not *freeloading*, photographers. There's no amount of advice, consultation, or even prayer that'll make you successful if you don't know the craft.

Don't expect clients to pay you while you practice on their jobs, wasting their time and money. If you know you can't handle an assignment, don't take it. That honesty will pay off in the long run.

If you feel it's necessary, start off slowly, and build your freelance business gradually while you gain experience. If you have the experience, then jump in with both feet!

Your income will depend on the amount of time you want to devote to your freelance business. A goal of $25,000 a year is completely reasonable. If you get into freelancing on a full-time basis, you can set your own top dollar volume. Even if you only work weekends, and a night every now and then, you should be able to earn $10,000 without any difficulty.

The freelance photography business is unlimited because you have the ability to create so much of the market and because you can establish your own rates. By selling your ideas and your work, you're making business where there was no business before, and opening up a whole new untapped world right at your doorstep.

Good reading, good luck, and may freelance photography bring you the joy and rewards it has brought me.

Chapter One

Homegrown, Hometown Freelance

(Your markets are right down the street)

Let's face it. If you're reading this book, you're interested in making money with your camera. You've probably read through several journals and books before getting to this one, looking for those money-making secrets.

If you're trying to find some magic formula in these pages that will tell you how to break into print in national magazines, national trade magazines, record jackets, and the like, then you'd better go back to your earlier reading. There's no magic here, only a workable plan to bring you extra cash if you're willing to follow and implement some proven methods.

Most of the books on freelance photography seem to have one thing in common: They assume that you cannot sell any photographs in your own hometown. To the authors of these books, freelance market means *faraway* market.

It's nice to dream of making the cover of *Ladies' Home Journal* or *People* or *Sports Illustrated*. It's fun to think that one day your photograph will be the record jacket for the latest pop smash. But for most of us, these are just dreams.

If you're the average photographer (and I'm not talking about ability) who wants to make a few extra bucks with his photographic knowledge, you need to think in more realistic terms. You must think not only in terms of what you can produce, but also in terms of what you'll be able to sell. If you don't, you could end up with a house full of rejects that aren't worth a plugged nickel to you or anybody else.

Those among us whom I classify as "photographic idealists" or "purists" have spent a great deal of their time in recent years arguing for an "art" status for photography. Indeed, there are times and situations when I, too, consider photography an art, but unfortunately the arty aspect of the medium doesn't produce revenue, except in rare instances to the very few who've made it to the top in the profession. These few professionals can afford to deal in art photography because they have the buyers for their work.

The rest of us must deal realistically with what will sell for us. We cannot afford the luxury of trying to convince the average customer that he needs a piece of *art* instead of a *picture* to help sell his product.

The abstract illusions, the far-out photographic essays, the dreamlike misty-graphs that have filled the pages of the photography magazines for years are fine for those few photographers who are fortunate enough to work for and sell to the four or five markets that will buy such "art."

But Hank Nikon from Springville, Susie Canon from Omaha, and Pete Miranda from Toledo will probably never see the light of day in any of the top national publications. And if they do, it will probably be a one-shot deal that won't earn them a month's supply of film.

But you can make money with your photography *right where you live*—not in some far-off magazine market. My own career is proof that you can earn a living right in your own hometown—even if it does happen to be miles from nowhere!

I've lived, and worked as a freelance photographer, in a town as small as 4,500 and in one as large as 130,000. I made money in both of them. I got $5 for the first photo I ever sold. The most I've ever been paid for a single photograph is $350. I got the same thrill out of both of those sales. The point is that I was being paid for what I created with my camera. You can do the same thing. One of the great joys of being a freelance photographer is that you never know when that phone rings whether it's just another $25 job or whether it might be that $1,000 job you've always been hoping for.

Believe me, there *are* $1,000 jobs in your city or town. They may not come along often, but they're there, and it doesn't take many of them to really give your income a boost!

Homegrown Freelance

When I was fifteen, I got a new camera for Christmas. I'll never forget that old Argus C-3, which at that time seemed to me to be the finest camera the world had ever known. I had to take it to a friend who worked at the drugstore so that he could load it with film.

There was something special about that camera and about that first roll of film. I was lucky enough (in later years I sometimes wondered whether it was luck) to sell a photo from that first roll to my hometown newspaper. All of a sudden I was a professional photographer! And I was hooked on the profession for life.

My career has run the gamut—from taking pictures as a high

Whether the main street of your hometown has only two grocery stores and a gas station, or is more on the order of this one, you *can* make money from freelance photography. How much you can make is limited only by the amount of time and effort you want to devote to your business.

school kid, to freelancing to help pay for my college education, to full-time freelancing, to owning my own photography studio for eleven years.

That Tiny Magazine Market

I guess I've read just about every book I could find to learn how to make money from photography. I've also read the photography magazines for all these years. What has amazed me most is the fact that all the books and most of the articles seem to be telling me to take photographs on speculation, mail them to some far-off magazine, and then sit back and wait to get that handsome check for my efforts. They don't bother to tell me that many of those magazines have their own staff photographers and that for every photo they buy from a freelancer, there are probably five thousand submissions they don't buy.

In other words, there are thousands of freelancers all over the country happily mailing in their work to what turns out to be a mighty small market. I tried going that route. I submitted travel pictures to big-city newspapers, human interest photos to the big-name magazines, and technical photos to the trade journals. And then there were the photo contests sponsored by some of the photography magazines. I never sold a thing.

I never was able to figure out how so many people were able to make money going around taking pictures of wrought-iron gates and fences, pigeons on a ledge, park benches from ten thousand different angles, and people with sad, heavily lined faces or funny-looking masks.

I finally realized that if I wanted to make money with my camera, I would have to take photos that would sell—and sell locally! I would have to be what I classify as a hometown freelancer.

Hometown Freelance

Now don't get me wrong. To be a hometown photographer doesn't mean you have to have a fine studio with elegant furniture, plenty of glass showcases, and framed 20x24s all over the walls. It's just the opposite; you don't have to have any studio at all. With a camera or two, a couple of strobe units, light stands, and a black-and-white darkroom setup, you're in business as a freelancer. You can go to the customer just as easily as he can come to a studio.

But let's not forget the most important asset, one you *must* have: the ability to use the above equipment to make a good photograph.

People are more than willing to pay for your work if you produce results they can use. They don't want and won't pay for fuzzy-graphs, or speckle-graphs, or photos that don't tell their story.

I'm assuming that you already are a photographer and that you know something of lighting, exposure, composition, and black-and-white darkroom procedures. In other words, you know how to turn out a salable photograph. My purpose here is to help you to sell what you already know how to produce.

A Craft Note

Before you offer your services for public consumption, and for pay, make sure you know your craft. If you're still learning the basics, and you're offered a job that you don't think you can handle, *pass it up!* Explain your reasons to the client. He'll respect you for it, and he won't forget you when the next job rolls around, because he knows that if you tell him you'll do it, *you can.*

People will gain confidence in you when you *act* like you know what you're doing. If you get into an awkward situation (maybe your battery is a little weak, and you have to keep a group standing there a minute or two until your ready light comes on and you can get the second shot), joke with them. Tell them that when you get paid for this job, you'll be able to afford a fresh battery, and you won't have to keep them waiting the next time. Never start offering apologies or fumbling around with the equipment as if you're trying to fix something.

If you do happen to mess up on a shot (and we all do from time to time), reshoot it. Deliver the good prints and explain to the client that you've given him a discount to make up for the inconvenience you caused him by missing the shot the first time.

A Little or a Lot

How much money can you make from freelance photography? You'll have to answer that question. I'd say the only limits on your dollar volume will be set by how hard you work at freelancing and how much time you want to devote to it. $25,000? You can do it. $15,000? Won't take a whole lot of effort. $10,000? It'll be a breeze!

If you work actively on a full-time basis, then you can make more than a decent living. If you work part-time, then you can supplement your other income significantly. The jobs are out there waiting for you. Whether you live in a rural community, small village, medium-sized town, or large city, there are money-making opportunities all around you, and you'll learn all about them in the chapters that follow.

Chapter Two

Let's Talk About Equipment

(Not a lot—just the right kind)

Quality photographic equipment is expensive; it always has been, and it always will be. The thought of this expense has kept many people from tackling the freelance market. Even though they consider themselves pretty good photographers, they figure they'll never be able to afford all the cameras, lenses, lighting equipment, and tremendous assortment of paraphernalia they've seen the "pros" carrying around.

This is another of the popular misconceptions about freelance photography. Too many people seem to think that if you don't have a telephoto lens a yard and a half long, or a fish-eye lens wide enough to capture the entire height of the Washington Monument from three feet away, you can't be a pro.

They've been taught by the photo magazines that you've got to have at least four cameras hung around your neck and three more in the bag for instant accessibility. You've got to have tripods that will support the weight of a compact car, two suitcases full of filters, a station wagon full of lighting equipment, and a travel trailer that contains all the other gadgets you might need.

Is that what the "experts" have convinced you that you need?

Bunk!

You know the definition of a photography expert, don't you? That's anybody with a camera bag who's more than a hundred miles from home.

In thirty-one years of selling on the freelance market, I'd venture to say that 90 percent of my photographs have been taken with a *normal lens* (80mm) on a hand-held 2¼ reflex camera. For the great majority of my artificial-light photos, I use a single strobe, either hand-held or bounced out of an umbrella. I do have a 50mm wide-angle lens for my 2¼ camera, and a 105mm lens for portraits (although I've shot many portraits with the normal lens).

All my photographic equipment fits quite nicely beside me on the front seat of my compact car—except the darkroom, and I could put all that in a hatchback and still have room for luggage. You don't have to have a lot of equipment, just the right equipment. Some of the poorest photographers I've ever met spent so much time studying new equipment and figuring out how to get the money to buy it that they couldn't concentrate enough to take a decent photograph. They're just like some fishermen I know. They buy every new lure that comes out every year, but they still can't catch fish.

How good a freelance photographer you are is *not* determined by how much equipment you own. I know one photography professor who made his advanced class spend the entire first month of their course using nothing but pinhole or old-fashioned box cameras. After much complaining, the students absolutely amazed themselves with the great photographs they were able to make with this rudimentary equipment. They concentrated on their subject and not on high-technology equipment. They were taking photographs, not operating computers.

The equipment discussed in the following sections is what I'm currently using, and have been using for at least twelve years. I've never run across a job I couldn't handle with this equipment, and I don't bother to haul it all along on most of my jobs. When I do take everything, the whole works will fit into one attaché-size metal camera case and one small leather gadget bag (everything, that is, except a couple of light stands and a tripod and umbrella, and they'll clip onto the outside of the gadget bag with a couple of leather straps).

Cameras

Three will do quite nicely. You could get by with two, but three will give you the capability to handle practically anything.

First, you'll need a 35mm single-lens reflex. I mention this first, not because it's my favorite, but because it's the smallest.

You'll find that most of your customers don't consider photos with grain or the least amount of fuzziness or poor definition to be art! They want photographs that are sharp and clear and detailed. For this reason I shoot very little black-and-white with my 35mm camera, preferring to work with a somewhat bigger negative. As you know, when you enlarge a 35mm negative to 8x10, any error is enlarged many times and becomes quite obvious. A similar error on a 2¼x2¼ negative is enlarged much less than 50 percent as much as on a 35mm negative.

My 35mm (which, by the way, is a Canon) is used primarily for color slides. I use it for black-and-white for some newspaper sports shots and news shots, some copy work that doesn't need to be enlarged a great deal, and some general newspaper assignments.

The workhorse of my equipment is a 2¼x2¼ camera. I prefer a

twin-lens reflex—the Mamiya C330—but many of my contemporaries like the 2¼ single-lens reflex.

I've found the C330 to be one of the most versatile cameras ever designed. With its extension bellows, it's excellent for detailed copy work. I use it for portraits, weddings, proms, newspaper assignments, commercial and industrial jobs—even aerials.

Lens changes are quite simple and fast on the C3330, the viewfinder is bright, the scales are easy to read, and it's durable. A little on the hefty side, but durable.

For years I got by with just these two cameras, and I could now if I had to. I did add a third camera to my inventory some time ago, an old Mamiya Press camera. The important thing here is the 2¼x2¾ format. I find this slightly bigger negative and its rectangular shape ideal for group photographs, and I now use this camera for almost all my aerials. It's easier to hold out the window of a small airplane than the C330, and its bigger negative is an important factor. When you're a thousand feet in the air, you're covering a lot of territory with every shot. This larger negative will be invaluable in clearly showing detail on the ground from your lofty perch.

The Mamiya Press is also great for color transparencies, which

These are the author's three working cameras, referred to many times throughout the book. They all fit in the sturdy, foam-lined camera case, which has saved them much abuse in travel from one job to another. The cameras are (left to right) Mamiya Press, Canon 35mm, and Mamiya C330.

are used instead of the smaller 35mm transparencies in the production of postcards and brochures.

With these three cameras, I guarantee that you'll be able to handle every situation.

Miniature Carry-Everywhere 35mm Cameras. I lied!

I've now got four cameras. But one is so much fun to play with, I really consider it more of a toy than a camera. Miniature 35mm cameras are a lot of fun, easy to handle, and great for a quick "grab" shot when you need one. My little "toy" camera goes just about everywhere I go. I've even used it on some jobs in a pinch.

Many of these miniature 35mm cameras have a semi-wide-angle lens (usually around 40mm). The depth of field is great, and the lenses themselves are sharp enough if you aren't going to blow up the prints to a very large size.

Some cameras are completely automatic, while others can be used this way or completely on manual. Mine has the shutter-priority system; I just dial in the ASA and the shutter speed I want to use, and it sets the correct f-stop. If you'd rather let the camera choose the shutter speed, while you control the f-stop, you can buy a camera with aperture priority.

There's a hot shoe for a small strobe unit, which can also be used on automatic. As you focus, the correct f-stop is set for you. There's also a plug-in jack for a regular strobe.

The primary reason I bought my little miniature 35mm is because I do quite a bit of fishing, and it fits like a glove in the bottom drawer of my tackle box. With that 40mm lens, which gives you a semi-wide-angle effect, it's great for shooting in the close confines of a fourteen-foot fishing boat.

By the way, I've sold some photos to other fishermen who had catches they were proud of. I just happened along, and happened to have a camera in my tackle box.

Cameras of this type are great to use for teaching purposes, if you have a spouse or child who wants to learn the business. The camera I have can be used on fully automatic or fully manual. You can start your pupils off on fully automatic, then as you teach them the purposes of shutter speeds and f-stops, they can begin trying manual operation.

This kind of camera is also great to carry along on a job as a backup in the event your primary equipment fails.

Another great advantage is that when an amateur slides up to you and says "What f-stop are you using?" you can honestly tell him you don't know; the camera is picking it for you. He'll figure you don't know any more than he does, and he'll slither up to somebody else. "Hey, buddy, what's your f-stop?" I love it! (I've thought about printing up a sign to wear that says, "My f-stop is 1,893.05," but I've never gotten around to it.)

Extra Lenses

Here's where you can save yourself a bunch of money. I hear people talking all the time about 1.1 or 1.2 or 1.4 lenses. What a waste of money just to be able to brag about the opening—and bragging is about all it's good for in our type of work. I recall using an f-stop larger than 2.8 only once, and I really had to stop and think about that time. If the available light is so bad that you have to shoot at 1/30 or 1/15 at f/1.1 or f/1.2 or f/1.4, you won't produce a picture your client will pay for anyway. Put some of your own light on the subject and shoot it at a decent shutter speed and f-stop.

For my 35mm camera I have a 35mm wide-angle lens and a 200mm telephoto lens that a guy sold me for twenty-five dollars. I use the wide-angle occasionally. I've used the telephoto a couple of times to shoot football and baseball for the newspaper, but never on any other kind of job. I play with it a lot, though.

I don't have any extra lenses for the Mamiya Press, only the 90mm normal lens that comes with it.

Light Meter

It doesn't have to be expensive, just good enough to read light. My 35mm camera has a built-in match-needle exposure meter. I use it most of the time and leave my other one at home.

Strobes

I own two strobe units: Both are old Braun RL 510s. That's the extent of my artificial lighting. They give me an f-stop of 16 at ten feet with Verichrome Pan or Plus-X film, f/22 with Tri-X. That's all I need. I'm not impressed with units that are "automatic" or that use rechargeable batteries, although I know many people who use them. I prefer to rely on my own judgment and on a battery that I know won't decide it wants to be recharged in the middle of a job.

Light Stands and Umbrellas

Also included in my lighting equipment are two silver umbrellas. I use regular light stands to hold the umbrellas, plus two slightly heavier light stands and a closet pole to support a portable roll-paper background. I'll talk more about this in Chapter 8.

Sync Cords—Carry a Spare

One extra that I always take along on any job is a spare sync cord. I've always had more trouble with them than any other type of equipment. If you get in a situation where your strobe won't fire, the first thing to do is to put on another sync cord. Nine times out of ten that will solve your problem.

And for goodness' sake, throw the old one away—*immediately.* You can't tell a good sync cord from a bad one by looking at it, and it's easy to mix them up. You won't be helping yourself if you take two bad cords on a job.

Speaking of extras, when I'm photographing an important job (well, they're all important, but some you can't stage over again), such as a wedding, I also take along an extra camera and strobe, just in case.

An extension sync cord is also a "must" when you're working with umbrellas, otherwise you'll be crouched in the umbrella with your regular-length cord.

Tripod

I have just one; it's a sturdy, but not heavy, model. You want a tripod that will adequately support your camera and won't wobble. But *you're* not going to be sitting on it, the camera is, and how many ounces does your camera weigh? Just look for a tripod with sturdy extension legs, and a head that tilts and swings would be nice, too.

Filters

There are at least three filters that you'll find useful in some situations. When shooting daylight color film indoors with available fluorescent light, you'll need a fluorescent-light filter to keep things from going green. You also may have need for a tungsten-light filter. A polarizing filter helps sometimes in eliminating reflections in glass.

I run into many people who keep a UV or haze filter on their 35mm camera lenses at all times. When I ask why, they always tell me someone at the camera store, or one of their friends who is a "pro," told them they should do it because it would give them better pictures and also protect their lens in case something should bang into it.

Well, in my opinion, this is absolutely foolish. In the first place, a filter is just another piece of glass that you have to worry about keeping clean in addition to keeping the lens clean. And if you ever bump into anything hard enough to damage that lens, you're going to break the filter anyway, and the broken glass will probably do a lot more damage to the lens than the bump would.

Keeping such a filter on your lens won't affect the quality of your photographs in any negative way, unless the filter itself is dirty or scratched. It's just an extra expense as far as I'm concerned.

Gadgets

You don't need them, but I buy them all the time. I'm what you might call a gadget freak. I don't buy them because they're necessary in my work; I just like to play with gadgets.

Even though photography has been my business for many years, I still like to *play* with it. Perhaps that's the reason I still enjoy my job so; the fun has never gone out of it.

There are all manner of *things*—table-top tripods, sparkle filters, cheap little strobe units, chains and straps, extension handles for strobe units, camera handles—and they're fun, if you can afford them. But they're not necessary for your work.

Used Equipment

Nobody ever said all your equipment had to be new. Some of the cameras I like aren't even made anymore, but they're still available on the used-equipment shelf in your camera shop, at pawn shops, or from individuals.

You've got to know what you're looking for, though, and know enough about cameras to make sure the used ones are working or can be repaired. When looking at used equipment, I always take some film along with me. I've yet to find a pawn shop operator or an individual who wouldn't let me load up the camera and shoot a roll of film right there on the spot. I always process the film before I make a deal.

Believe it or not, some freelance photographers fail. Some aren't good enough and some just get tired of it. I enjoy reading the newspaper classified ads, and I always check to see if there are any freelancers going out of business.

One time, because there was one camera listed that I wanted, I answered an ad that must have included thirty or forty items. The seller was a rich "serious amateur" who decided he was fed up with photography. He offered me the entire lot for a price that was ridiculously low. I bought everything he had, then resold everything I'd bought except the one camera I had originally wanted.

What About Film?

I try to keep my film list simple. In the 120 size I use Tri-X and Verichrome Pan for black-and-white. I like the old Verichrome Pan when I don't need the extra speed. For color prints I use Kodacolor 400 (CG) or Vericolor II (VPS). In 35mm I use Tri-X or Plus-X, again depending on the speed I need for the job. I rarely use 35mm color print film, but when I do it's CG. I use high speed Ektachrome (EL) for all size transparencies. All of these films are manufactured by Kodak.

My one admonition about film is to always carry more than you think you're going to need on a job. It's mighty embarrassing when the client thinks of a couple of extra shots he forgot to tell you about, and you have to inform him that you just ran out of film. There isn't always a drugstore handy where you can run in and pick up another roll, and if you do find a drugstore, you might not be getting fresh film.

When you're shooting something like a prom or a dance school, you never know in advance exactly how many rolls of film you'll need. It's a hard decision to make, especially if your funds are limited and you're just buying film for that one particular job, but you can really lose money if you take too little.

Where can you get the best deal when you buy film? It depends more or less on where you live. Most photography stores will give a 20 percent discount on supplies to professional photographers, but you'll have to ask for it. If you live in a city large enough to have a photo equipment wholesaler, you can buy direct. If you live in a small town or rural area, it might be well worth your time to visit the closest large city and set up an account with a wholesaler or a large photo store. Then you can order your materials and have them delivered by mail.

I've never ordered film through ads in the photography magazines, but I have ordered paper from them and been well pleased with the service.

Film Storage

Especially with color film. I always store my on-hand supply in the refrigerator. This will definitely extend the shelf life. But don't store any film this way on which you've broken the foil wrap. I just put the boxes right in the refrigerator, usually in the "butter keeper." You don't need to wrap the boxes in anything extra.

Take the film out an hour or two before you intend to use it so it can warm up to room temperature. Put the cold film in a small plastic bag, seal it, and let it warm up. This will keep condensation to a minimum. If you use it cold, there could well be a lot of condensation forming on the film.

Battery Storage

My strobe units take the 510-volt dry cell. I always keep one or two on hand. This might be especially advisable in a small-town or rural situation where these batteries have to be specially ordered.

I keep my spares in the freezer, again for the purpose of extending shelf life. (Again, no extra wrap is necessary. The box the battery comes in provides all the protection you need.) You won't have to worry about a spare battery that you may have had for six months or longer if you keep it frozen. Allow several hours for it to thaw out.

Masking Tape

Other than a couple of lens shades and a little screwdriver repair kit, there you have my equipment list.

I did forget one item. *Masking tape!* Never go anywhere on a job without a roll of masking tape. You'll never know how many things you'll need to use it for. I've used it to hold equipment together, to hold people and other subjects together, to hold backgrounds in place, to hold a horse's ear erect, to hold a child's favorite toy in front of the camera, and even to mark a spot on the floor.

You can get by with only two cameras, but never try to skimp on masking tape!

Chapter Three

What About a Darkroom?

(It doesn't have to be big)

My darkroom is four feet by eight feet. That's really a little too small, but I've gotten by with it all these years. If I had it to do over again, I would make it a trifle larger; however, it sure has saved me a lot of walking! Matter of fact, I can't walk in there at all, just shuffle around a bit.

I process only black-and-white film. This capability is a must for any freelancer. A good part of your work will be in black-and-white. There are photo labs all over the country that process color, but have you seen any advertisements lately for black-and-white processing? Surely you don't want to go to drugstore processing, so about the only answer is to do it yourself.

Besides, this will give you far better quality control, plus the convenience of being able to do the work on a time schedule that'll make your clients happy. Many clients expect to have to wait for color prints because they realize most photographers send color work off to labs, but they don't want to wait a week or more for black-and-white jobs.

Another reason why I process black-and-white and don't process color is the expense involved in the equipment necessary for good color production. Why should I invest my money (and a sizable chunk of it at that) in order to have enough color processing equipment just to get by, when I can use a color lab that has invested hundreds of thousands of dollars in the best equipment, methods, and personnel? It's much cheaper to pay them to do it, in terms of both cost and time. I can put my time to better use selling and shooting.

Equipment

As I've said, you don't have to have a lot of space, but running water is *not* a luxury. I've known quite a few photographers who started off using a bathroom for a darkroom, and it's not really a bad setup with a little bit of preplanning. If you have a counter large enough to hold an enlarger, that's fine. If not, you can cut a piece of plywood to fit over the bathtub or lavatory to hold the enlarger. The shower curtain rod makes an excellent place to hang film to dry. You can buy a little rubber gadget that fits over the drain of the tub or lavatory to convert it to a circulating print washer.

Some weather stripping or tape can seal the cracks around the door to take care of light leaks. If there's a window in your bathroom, you can buy light-blocking window shades, or use a piece of heavy, dark cloth or wood. Working at night makes blocking up a window considerably easier.

My darkroom contains a sink, an Omega D-2V enlarger (which will handle negatives from 35mm through 4x5), four trays, a print washer, a Lott rotary drum dryer (which will take six 8x10s at a time, or two 11x14s).

I also have a safelight, an enlarger timer, and a wind-up timer for film processing. I have two stainless steel tanks, assorted 35mm and 120 reels, an enlarging easel, a paper cutter, a thermometer—and that's it. Again, I haven't invested a whole lot of money, but what equipment I have is adequate to do the job.

I've gone almost entirely to RC paper, and in the event you travel this route, you'll have no need for a print dryer. RC paper is also a real time-saver during washing, and it gives a nice, even gloss with no spots, wrinkles, or curls.

Another convenient piece of equipment to have is a drying cabinet for film, especially when you need to develop a roll and get a quick print. Drying cabinets are expensive if you purchase a commercial model; however, I just finished making my own for very little money.

I purchased enough twelve-inch shelving board to make a box one foot square by six and a half feet high (to accommodate 36-exposure rolls of 35mm film). I hinged one side for the door, in which I left a three-inch opening at the top to help with air circulation. About six inches from the bottom, I nailed small strips of wood to support a piece cut from an air conditioner filter. Under this I put an old hair dryer. Presto—warm, filtered air, which rises from the bottom and exits the top, giving me an even drying process that doesn't curl the film. The drying cabinet fits perfectly in the corner of the room, taking up very little useful space.

Your Chemicals

The first and most important rule for using chemicals is to follow the directions on the label. This is true both for mixing and for using them to achieve the desired results. For instance, if you don't mix chemicals thoroughly so that all particles are completely dissolved, you could end up with spots or streaks on your film and prints. If you leave prints in the fixer too long, they might have a tendency to curl.

Buying chemicals in gallon rather than quart sizes is much more economical, even if you're afraid you might have trouble using up an entire gallon before it goes bad. One solution is to store the chemicals in dark-colored bottles. They'll have a longer shelf life after mixing if you keep light away from them. You can buy plastic chemical bottles, but I always prefer to get bottles from a druggist. Some liquid medicines come in gallon glass bottles that are a dark brown. These are ideal for photo chemicals, and they're usually free—if you know the druggist.

Be sure to wash the bottles thoroughly. Many times a heavy, syruplike liquid comes in them and it will crystallize or become very gummy in the bottom. I use a regular dishwashing detergent and warm water. Let it soak for a while and rinse thoroughly.

A word about stop bath: I don't use it. I've found that it creates more problems for me than it solves. I use a tray of plain water, which I change frequently while I'm printing, and plain water in my film-developing tank as a rinse before adding fixer.

Don't attempt to stretch the life of your chemicals by processing just one more roll of film or squeezing in one more print. Exhausted chemicals will show up in your print quality every time.

Try to stay close to the recommended temperatures for your chemicals and wash water. In the winter, you can raise the temperature of your chemicals by setting the tank or tray in a larger tray of hot water. In the summer, you can reduce the temperature by putting ice cubes in a plastic bag and immersing the bag in your tank or tray. As you know, temperature isn't nearly as critical in black-and-white processing as it is in color, but try to stay close to the recommended range.

Stabilization Processing

One piece of equipment that I don't have, but have seriously considered purchasing, is a stabilization processor. It would save considerable time in printing and would be especially helpful for such things as newspaper photos, which are no longer needed once the newspapers have been printed. Stabilization-processed prints are good for at least six months or longer. If you need to make them permanent, then you can put them through regular acid fixer and a wash, and you've got permanent prints. Since there's an RC stabilization paper, you'd still have no need for a print dryer.

While these processors were very expensive for a while, there are now models on the market which are priced in the reasonable range. Stabilization chemistry is a little more expensive than regular chemistry, but paper cost is about the same.

With a portable enlarger and a stabilization processor, you could set up a darkroom just about anywhere. You've practically eliminated the need for running water. One friend of mine who does a lot of travel articles has such a setup in his mini-motor home.

Foot and Leg Comfort

If your darkroom has a concrete floor like mine, your feet and legs can get mighty tired from a long day or night of processing and printing.

I solved this problem by buying one of those foam-rubber-backed household mats. Believe me, it makes a difference. I think those were about the best few dollars I ever spent.

Another help for tired legs is to work in crepe-sole shoes, especially when on assignment. You never know when you're going to be climbing on top of furniture, cabinets, cars, or whatever in order to get the shot you need. Not only are such shoes more comfortable, but they provide surer and safer footing as well.

Processing for Other People

Since there aren't many professional black-and-white labs around anymore, having your own could well mean that you'll also be able to pick up some custom processing work for people who can't do their own.

I have several such accounts, including the public relations office for a school district, some state government agencies that have photographers but not their own darkroom, and some serious amateur photographers who are willing to pay for professional handling of their black-and-white film.

When it comes to this kind of processing, people without their own facilities are faced with using either freelancers like myself or the drugstore—enough said?

My black-and-white processing prices aren't cheap, but I take pride and care in what I turn out for my customers. I work with each of my processing customers on an individual basis, in many cases giving them overnight service when they need it (and when I can do it that quickly without sacrificing something else that has to be done). I never charge any more for rush service, and my customers know that the few times I have to tell them I can't get a rush order out, there's good reason for it. If I charged more for rush service, then I'd be obligated to turn the order out regardless of what other work I had.

There have been times when I didn't actively seek freelance assignments because I had so much black-and-white processing coming in. If you turn out quality work, the word will spread quickly. I even have some camera stores and drugstores referring customers to me when they feel the customer wants better work than their normal automated processing will produce.

Processing can quickly become an important revenue-producing activity if you're interested. It's something that you can usually work into your off-hours. One advantage of having a darkroom in your home is that you can be doing something else while you're waiting for film to develop and negatives or prints to wash and dry.

I've known some photographers who've built just about their entire business on processing for other people. While prices vary widely, the $6-to-$10 range is not uncommon for processing a roll of film and making a proof sheet. Add anywhere from $4 to $8 for an 8x10 print, $2 to $5 for a 5x7 print. You can see how any volume at all will give you a good income from processing. Of course, you'll have to base your prices on what the traffic will bear in your area—but remember, you're providing *custom* black-and-white processing. You should give your customer the best possible print you can from the negatives, without dust spots and stains and scratches and streaks. If you're going to charge a lot more than the drugstore, you'll have to provide much better results.

Using a Hole Punch to Identify Film. If you're processing several rolls of film for other people and don't know the subject matter, here's an easy way to identify each roll. Buy yourself one of those old-fashioned hole punches, the kind they use to punch lunchroom or dance hall tickets. Punch a certain number of holes in the order envelope, then a corresponding number of holes in the leader of each roll of film that goes with that order, a different number of holes for the next order, and so on.

Labs accomplish the same purpose with printed number tags, but I've found that the hole punch works just as well and is much cheaper.

Color Processing

In some cases I can buy color prints from a lab cheaper than the prices I charge customers for custom black-and-white prints. But these color prints are machine-processed, automated cheapies. Don't get me wrong; they're fine for some things, but they aren't the quality, hand-printed, dodged, spotted prints that you get when you pay much higher prices for custom work.

Machine or automated prints are fine for such things as proms, Little League teams, dance schools, etc. There's nothing wrong with such prints if you don't lead the customer to expect the niceties of hand-printed, custom, portrait-type work. You can make a handsome profit on machine-processed prom sets, and give your customers something they'll be proud of for the price. If you take some care in composition and shooting and deal with a lab that will handle your work carefully, you'll get results you won't be ashamed to deliver.

Your best bet is to shoot a test roll and send it in to the lab for the type of machine processing you intend to order from that establishment. I've found that most good labs are consistently good, and most bad ones are consistently bad. The good labs, if they do mess up occasionally, will print remakes without any hassle at all. Just return the bad prints in the original order envelope and ask them to do it over, for whatever reason.

Listed here are some of the color labs that I've used on a regular basis over the years. Just because a lab isn't listed here doesn't mean that I have anything against them. I've probably never tried them out. But the following I know from personal experience:

Garrett & Lane Color Laboratories
Box 5608
Columbus GA 31906

Cameo Color, Inc.
1700 W. Diversey Parkway
Chicago IL 60614

Meisel Photochrome Corporation
Box 226067
Dallas TX 75222

Being able to communicate with any lab is extremely important, whether you use written instructions on your order or call to discuss a particular job. It's also nice to know that when the lab has a question about your work, someone will go to the trouble to call you.

All of the labs listed have booklets detailing their services, prices, etc. They'll also provide you with order envelopes, negative sleeves, and mailing boxes.

Chapter Four

Business Basics

(Freelancing is more than taking pictures)

It would be great if all you had to do to run a freelance photography business was to enjoy shooting photographs and working in the darkroom. The most enjoyable part of it for me is being behind the camera and working with my clients. But somewhere along the line we have to determine where the art of being a photographer leaves off and the discipline of being a business person begins.

You can be the best photographer in the world, but if you don't know something about operating the business end of the enterprise, you're in for trouble. You may find it distasteful to have to sit down and figure out bills, push past-due accounts for payment, do your paperwork. But you'll find out rather quickly that your creditors don't mind doing this where your business accounts are concerned. They'll demand their money on time, just as you should demand yours.

While you don't have to own your own studio and a lot of fancy equipment to be successful as a freelance photographer, there are a few simple and inexpensive items that should help your work (like a tape recorder, which I'll explain later in this chapter). There are also some practical business matters for you to consider, such as having a special bank account to keep your business financial records separate from your personal affairs.

Now, none of the items mentioned will automatically make you a better freelance photographer. But I've found over the years that some initial investments—like hiring a CPA to set up your books correctly—will pay for themselves many times over. Some of my suggestions are just that, suggestions, like the one about buying a tape recorder. Others, like my admonition to always carry a camera no matter what you're doing, are born out of my own misfortunes—for example, those once-in-a-lifetime shots that got away.

Let's get started with the area that's perhaps the most interesting—and frustrating—money!

Fees

I'll make a confession to you right at the beginning to set the record straight. The one aspect of being a freelance photographer that has always given me problems has been setting my fees—determining how much to charge my clients. Throughout this book I'll be making suggestions for how to price your work, what kind of packages seem to work best, etc., based on my experience.

The principle that I've always tried to follow when setting fees is to be fair both to myself and to my client. My goal is not to give my work away, nor is it to sock it to the person for whom I'm working; rather, it's to determine what amount will adequately compensate me for my time, talent, and investment in equipment for any particular job.

Believe it or not, I've heard freelance photographers say, "I can afford to charge less for my work than a studio because I don't have any

This aerial view includes shopping centers, banks, schools, churches, restaurants, discount stores, homes, dance schools, real estate agencies, manufacturing plants—every one a potential customer for your freelance photography business.

overhead." What an idiotic statement! I don't care if you're using a camera that Uncle Charlie willed to you, driving a car that you picked up at the junkyard, and operating out of the family home that was paid for before the Great Depression—everyone in business has overhead!

You have expenses for photo supplies, depreciation on your photo equipment, business licenses, taxes, office supplies, advertising, operating your automobile, darkroom equipment, and water and electricity to operate your darkroom. This is only a small part of what sometimes seems like an endless list of expenses you'll incur. So don't let anyone ever convince you that you don't have overhead the way the studios do.

What you charge for your work is something that you'll ultimately have to determine for yourself based on the area you live in and its economy, what your competition charges, and last but not least, how much money you need or want to make from your business.

There are basically two ways to set your fees:

Per photo or per job. You can charge per individual photograph, or per individual job. If you set a fee per photograph, you may want to negotiate a price on a job that includes many different shots. This type of pricing includes darkroom work and expenses involved in the job.

By the hour. You can determine a charge for your time and talent in shooting photographs on an hourly basis. This hourly rate will only cover your time spent in actual shooting and in setting up the shots. All darkroom work and expenses are extra. You'll charge extra for every roll of film you shoot, process, and proof, and for every print you deliver to the client. Hourly rates are also usually "portal to portal"—meaning your charges start when you leave your home or place of business and continue until you finish the job and return to your home or place of business.

Both methods have their advantages and disadvantages, and there are some jobs which necessitate using one or the other. For instance, when you're shooting prom sets or packages for dance schools, Little League teams, or school dances (all of these are covered in upcoming chapters), there's no way you can charge by the hour. You have to set a specific price per set of photos. When you're shooting fashion shots for a local department store, it may take the store personnel and models an hour or more to set up for one shot. It would be foolish in this circumstance to charge on a per-photo basis, when you have no idea how long the job will take.

When quoting a price per photo or job, you know in advance exactly how much you are going to make every time you shoot. If it takes you two minutes to do a shot, then you're being paid handsomely for those two minutes—plus the darkroom time involved. But suppose that shot were more complicated than you first suspected, and it took you the better part of an hour to get it on film. In that case you wouldn't have been paid nearly as well for the time you spent on it.

On the other hand, if you charge an hourly rate, then you know you're going to make a specific amount per hour—even if the client is slow in getting the equipment in place or the models dressed. You'll also be getting paid for your darkroom time through your charges for processing and proofing each roll of film and for making each print.

In the chapter on darkrooms, I discussed custom processing and printing that you can do for other photographers. When you're working on an hourly rate, your darkroom charges for clients should be exactly the same as your charges to other people for processing and proofing their film and making prints. You don't charge the client your hourly rate while you're working in the darkroom.

Also, when you're on an hourly rate, you may want to have a minimum charge of one hour per job, even for only one shot. Some photographers work this way and some break their time charges down into half-hour segments with a minimum charge of one half hour.

Day Rate. There's another method of charging which you may have occasion to use. Advertising agencies or big firms may ask you to work on a day rate instead of a per-photo or hourly rate.

To calculate your day rate, take your hourly rate and multiply it by the number of hours in the client's day; then reduce it by some percentage, say 10 percent. The amount of reduction is up to you.

Of course, all expenses are extra—mileage, meals, air transportation, etc. You'll also charge for each roll of film (remember, the price includes your charges for processing and proofing) and each print.

If you have a rather involved job which will take quite a bit of time, it might be best to charge your day rate. Let's say there might be a wait of an hour or two in some phases of the job. If you're on an hourly rate, the client might dismiss you during this time and you wouldn't get paid for it. And what could you do with that time but go somewhere, sit, and wait to go back and finish up? It probably wouldn't be enough time to go out and try to squeeze in another job. If you're on a day rate, you may still have to sit and wait, but at least you'll be getting paid for it.

Money in the Bank

Always have a separate business account for your freelance photography activities. It's much easier to keep track of your financial records that way. Come income tax time, you can use your canceled checks from the business account to verify your expenses.

Be sure to note on each check what it was for. If it's to pay invoices which are numbered, list these numbers on the check. This will be a big help if there's ever any question as to whether a certain invoice was paid. You should also keep all paid invoices on file for tax purposes.

Another record-keeping aid is to note on each invoice the check number and the date it was paid.

Happy income tax time! (Look on the bright side. If you're having to pay income tax on your freelance photography business, at least there was income.)

Income Tax Time. If you use a certain portion of your home for your business—as in the case of a darkroom, camera room, etc.—you can deduct a percentage of certain household expenses as business expenses. These include such expenditures as utilities, insurance, repairs, garbage collection (but don't try to deduct your food). In Internal Revenue Service jargon, this is called a "home office." There was a time when every traveling salesman, everybody on call at home after working hours, claimed a home office. The IRS has tightened up considerably on this provision, but if you're a legitimate freelancer, you should qualify. Check with your CPA.

If you qualify and, say, you devote 10 percent of the floor space in your home to your freelance business, then you can deduct 10 percent of your household expenses such as telephone bills, light and heating, water, garbage collection, repairs to the structure, and insurance. You can also take a certain amount of depreciation on your home. This could really be helpful, and it would pay you to check on it with your accountant. The same holds true if you rent your home or apartment. A portion of your expenses is deductible.

Your Accountant

If you have any kind of business volume at all, hire the services of an accountant to help you set up your books and do your income tax returns. I guarantee he'll save you more money than his fee will cost you.

My CPA established a set of books for me so that when I write each check, I'm also doing my bookkeeping. There's a ledger page underneath the sheet of checks. The checks have a carbon backing on the line where you write all the information and this is automatically transferred to the ledger sheet. The only extra information I have to add to the ledger are bank deposits.

There are things like tax credits for equipment purchased, depreciation on home and auto, depreciation on equipment—all kinds of ways an accountant can save you money or save you from having to pay a penalty and extra taxes.

You'll have to file a declaration of estimated income tax (form 1040-ES) unless your business is incorporated. If you're not incorporated, you can't pay yourself a salary and withhold Social Security and income tax.

Is it best to operate as a sole proprietorship or to incorporate the business? Should you elect Subchapter S? What about sales tax? Do you need a business license? What monthly tax forms must you submit? How detailed should your records be? How many years must you keep your records on file? Is it better to lease an automobile or buy one? Is it better to take a deduction on your automobile of so much per each mile you drive it, or should you take the deduction on the basis of actual expenses plus depreciation?

An accountant or CPA can answer such questions and save you lots of time, money, and trouble. Using one is a wise investment.

Business Licenses

If you purchase a business license for your operation in the city or town where you live, this doesn't mean that you're covered in any other city or town. Each municipality has its own business license, and you'll have to have a license for each one in which you do business.

In many cases local photographers are quite fussy about out-of-towners coming into their area and taking their business, especially weddings. I recall one instance when I journeyed to a nearby town to do a wedding. It just so happened that I had relatives living in this town, and they had warned me not to come in without a license. When I arrived at the church, there was a policeman waiting to check my license. Had I not had it, there would have been a $100 fine plus the cost of the license, which I would have had to purchase before I could shoot the wedding. This happened to be a Saturday, and naturally city hall was closed. Would you like to try to explain a situation like this to a bride who's getting ready to walk down the aisle?

You should also be aware that in some areas of the country there are county business licenses in addition to those required by the cities.

Insurance

Make sure you have adequate liability insurance! Especially for jobs involving possible risk to the client, like photographing a child on a pony (see Chapter 28). You never know when you might need such insurance, no matter how careful you are or how safe the job appears.

Also carry insurance on your equipment. In most cases this can be obtained cheaper, and just as effectively, through a rider on your home owner's policy, rather than a separate policy. Make certain, however, that your insurance agent knows the equipment is being used commercially. It will cost a little more for the coverage, but will be well worth the extra expense if the opportunity ever arises for you to collect on your insurance. You should also make certain that the policy will pay off even if the equipment was stolen from your car and the window wasn't broken or the door forced open. Then you won't have to prove that it was taken from a locked car, as some policies require.

The liability insurance coverage can also be obtained on your home owner's policy.

You know what they say about insurance: It ain't worth a dime— until you need it!

Identify Your Film

Sometime when you don't have anything better to do, stop by any post office and ask them to show you the unidentified rolls of film they've accumulated from film mailers that were torn open by a machine or not sealed properly. It's quite easy for film and envelopes to get separated, and there's no way for postal employees to tell who owns the film once it gets separated from its mailer. You can imagine the headaches, heartaches, and loss of revenue this can cost the unwary. What if this happened to one of your weddings or some other order that you could not restage and reshoot?

Years ago I started putting one of my address labels on each roll of film that I sent through the mail. There's never been a time when the post office has had to depend on my labels, but if it ever arises, they'll be able to identify my film.

You can buy little gummed address labels very cheaply. You've seen them advertised in practically every magazine you've ever read. Mail-order firms also offer the larger, self-stick address labels, which are slightly more expensive. Regardless of which type you choose, these labels are cheap insurance.

As another precaution, I always use strapping tape to reinforce envelope mailers at all corners where flaps are sealed over. I don't use masking tape or cellophane tape; the Postal Service only approves strapping tape.

Identify Your Photos

In addition, I always identify every photograph I deliver, usually with a rubber stamp or one of the self-stick address labels. For RC paper, you can buy quick-drying ink pads from any firm that makes up rubber stamps, or you can order them out of the classified section of any photography magazine.

Even though it's hard for you to imagine, sometimes clients do forget your name. It helps if they can flip over a photo from their last order and find it there along with your telephone number. It's also handy when a client shows your work to a friend or associate. The friend may make a mental note of your name and call you the next time he or she needs photographs.

Hate to Make Change?

When you're pricing your prom sets or group photos for dance schools, Little League teams, meetings, etc., where you collect at the time you shoot, try to come out to an even dollar. It's much simpler when you don't have to stop to count out change or carry rolls of nickels, dimes, and quarters around with you. Folding money is much nicer, and it doesn't weigh near as much.

On big jobs, when you'll be taking up a lot of money and shooting a lot of photos in a short time, take someone along with you to handle the money and write the receipts.

Speaking of receipts, it's good to always carry a receipt book in your camera bag or case. Every so often you'll run into someone who will pay you on the spot and in cash. I buy these books from the office supply store and prestamp them with my name and address on the signature line. Then I initial the receipt when I write it out.

It's always best to give a receipt when you're paid in cash whether or not the client requests one. This is for your protection as well as his.

Transportation and Parking

I've always preferred a compact hatchback. Not only does it get great gas mileage around town, which is a real savings, but it's easy to park, easy to handle, and easy to load with equipment. The hatchback feature even makes it ideal to haul around that roll-paper background and the ten-foot closet pole you use to hold it up. Try that in a regular sedan!

Parking can be a problem, especially when you have a job downtown. Wouldn't it be nice to be able to pull into a loading zone?

You can! In my city you can buy a loading zone permit for five dollars per year, and regardless of the vehicle, you can park in the loading zone—not for an extended stay, but certainly long enough to shoot a normal job. Not everyone can buy these permits; you have to have a logical need for one, and photographers meet this requirement.

The money you spend for a loading zone permit, even if it's more than five dollars where you live, can be a very time- and frustration-saving expenditure. Check with your police department; they issue the permits. You'll need to take along your vehicle's registration card and something to prove that you're in the photography business.

Luggage Rack Is Helpful. If you buy a car, compact or station wagon, a luggage rack on top comes in handy for hauling extra items. It also can function as a ready-made platform to give you that little extra height advantage you sometimes need on a job.

I use a piece of three-quarter-inch plywood, cut to fit on top of the rails of the luggage rack. Holes drilled in the wood are fitted with leather straps so it can be firmly attached to the rails to make a stable platform for shooting. It's big enough to hold me and a tripod if I need one up there. If you need even more height, it's also sturdy enough to support a stepladder. You can nail one-inch strips of wood to the plywood to provide stops to keep the ladder from sliding, and I use a ladder with rubber on the feet to make it even steadier. The ladder made for painters—with a rolled, curved bar at the top and an extended shelf in the front—is ideal for this type of work.

Tape Recorders

I like to carry one of the little compact tape recorders—the ones that use the minicassettes—in my camera case. They're very small, weigh only a few ounces, and don't take up much space at all.

When a client starts rattling off instructions on a particular photo he wants, and he won't be around when you're shooting, it's mighty easy to whip out your cassette recorder and press the button instead of fumbling for a pen and something to write on while he talks a mile a minute. Also, it eliminates questions about the client's instructions. If later he thinks that he gave different instructions from the ones you've followed, you can replay them for him.

While some of these recorders are quite expensive, there are cheaper ones on the market. The length of recording time you get on the tapes seems to be the determining factor in price. The cheaper ones only give you fifteen minutes on each side for a total of thirty minutes on the tape. The more expensive ones give you thirty minutes on each side for a total of one hour's recording time per tape.

If you're using the recorder just for notes, thirty minutes is plenty of recording time. However, if you're using it for newspaper interviews or the like, you'll need to go to the more expensive miniature, or a regular cassette recorder which uses the full-size cassettes. All of these will give you an hour's time. The larger cassettes are also less expensive than the minis.

Always Carry a Camera

Always! You never know when you're going to run into that once-in-a-lifetime shot. Suppose you really did come upon a sasquatch or a flying saucer!

If you happen on the scene of a wreck, you might be able to sell photos of it for insurance or legal purposes (see Chapters 15 and 24) or to the newspaper. The same is true of fires.

Along with the miniature 35mm cameras that are on the market now (see Chapter 2), it's easy enough to find a little plastic case that you can attach to your belt. Then you can carry a camera all the time. If your belt holds up as much as mine does, you surely aren't going to notice another four or five ounces. A woman can easily slip one of these cameras into her purse.

File a Flight Plan

Someone at home always knows where I am and how to get in touch with me, whether I'm out on an assignment, or just out.

You'd be surprised how many jobs come along that have to be done *right now* or not at all.

If you're out a great deal, very busy, and have a lot of clients who need to get in touch with you immediately, you may want to consider having a telephone put in your car, or using one of the page or "beeper" systems offered by telephone answering services. That way someone can always get a message to you.

I haven't invested in any of the above yet, but I'm considering it. Maybe if you get a few of your friends to buy copies of this book, I'll be able to afford one.

I've tried answering services but have never been pleased with the results. I've also tried one of the automatic answering devices you can put on your own phone. I still use this when there's no one at home, but you'd be surprised at the number of people who absolutely refuse to talk to a machine. It's better than nothing, though, and you'll get some messages. Spend the little extra money it takes to get a model which allows you to call in to your own phone and have the messages played back for you over the line. This way you can return important messages sooner without having to run home to listen to the machine.

Any of these suggestions will give you better communications with your customers and might also save you some money on gas! You know how important that is with today's petrol prices.

Each of the topics covered in this chapter can help you run your business more efficiently and effectively. Every penny you can save in operating expenses and in taxes is a penny you don't have to worry about earning.

But even the most efficient operation won't get off the ground unless you have business—and that business consists of clients and assignments. One way to find business opportunities is to advertise your services; I'll cover that in the next chapter.

Chapter Five

Advertising

(You can't sell it if you don't show it)

There are many opportunities, even in a small town, to display your work. The more people you show what you can produce, the more jobs you'll be called on to do. It's just that simple. I've run into some photographers who didn't want to spend any of their own money to have sample photographs printed, but I believe this is one of the cheapest and most effective types of advertising you can do.

I've run into other photographers who really understood the value of displaying sample prints, and who made it a point to always order two prints of any outstanding shot—one for the customer and one for display. Labs charge more for the first print on any custom order. That first-print price includes the setup charge, sample prints to check color balance, and other one-time costs. A second print ordered at the same time is always cheaper. This is why you should always order your sample prints when you place the customer's order.

I heard of one photographer who used his display prints both for promotion and to insure prompt payments from customers. If a customer hadn't paid, the photographer displayed the print upside down!

This photographer also said he ran his first newspaper advertisement upside down and got more than a thousand calls telling him that he had wasted his money running that ad. The photographer gave each one of those callers a sales pitch and ended up selling about half of them on having him do their photography.

A little innovation every now and then has never hurt any freelance photographer.

Obtaining Releases

In order to use a photograph of a person, someone's pet, or a recognizable building or piece of property for advertising purposes, you must have a signed model release. This is usually easy to obtain. Some studios incorporate a release in their standard contract form which the customer signs. This release authorizes the photographer to use any of the photos for samples and advertising.

If you don't have a contract form, most photography stores carry pads of printed model releases; all you have to do is fill in the blanks and get a signature. These pads are also advertised in most of the photography magazines. It's a very inexpensive investment to buy a pad of these releases and keep it in your camera bag. It's much easier to get a release signed when you take the photograph, rather than to find out at a later date that you have a sale for the photograph and can't remember who the person was or don't know how to get in touch with him.

Just be sure you get a release, or don't use that particular photograph. You don't want a lawsuit on your hands for unauthorized use of a photo. That will make advertising too expensive—regardless of the media you choose.

Banks

Many banks like to have displays of various types from time to time. Photographs make a very effective display, and all the prints don't have to be tremendous color prints, either. There's always a place for well-done black-and-white photos. Ask your bank about sponsoring a display of all the different types of work you do.

Another possibility is to suggest to the bank that you take "executive portraits" of all their top officers at work in their offices. The bank could then display these portraits in a show in the lobby before hanging them in other appropriate places.

Also suggest executive portraits of the members of the bank's board of directors, which later could be hung in the board room. Since members of the board always represent many of the leading businesses in the community, this could easily give you access to many different firms. I can't think of many better ways to get your foot in the door than by producing a dignified, pleasing portrait of the president of a firm.

These portraits could make up your entire display, or the executive portraits could be incorporated with others to show your versatility.

Of course, if the bank likes the executive portraits suggestion, you'll get paid for shooting them, besides having photos for a potential display.

Shopping Centers

Shopping centers offer many business opportunities (see Chapter 14). They also often feature displays and shows to attract and entertain customers. In many cases, there's no charge to the exhibitors in these shows. Shopping centers look on such displays as a way to take part in community activities while at the same time bringing in more shoppers.

Check with the director of the merchants' association of the shopping center about the possibility of having a display during the next art show, or talk them into having a photography show. If you have enough material, suggest that you have a show all your own. If you do this, make certain that you have a wide variety of photographs and include some of your best assignments—commercial and industrial shots, group and individual portraits, pet photos, aerial photos, still life and arty photographs, sports shots, dance school photos, wedding candids and bridal portraits, environmental (outdoor) portraits, and architectural shots. I'll be discussing many of these special subjects in upcoming chapters.

The secret of a successful display is to have quality photographs of many different kinds of subjects. The more the merrier; have something for everybody.

Portfolios

It's always nice to have a prepared portfolio of your work to show to potential clients. It should be made up of quality prints at least 8x10 inches in size, both color and black-and-white. It would be good to include some 11x14 prints as well. Each print should be attractively mounted. Some photographers prefer to mount 8x10 prints on 11x14 boards.

Include some 35mm slides in your portfolio. The best way to display these is to place them in 8½x11 plastic sheets, which usually hold twenty slides. These sheets are also available to hold 2¼x2¼ or 4x5 transparencies, if you have the capability of producing those sizes. Transparencies larger than 35mm are almost mandatory on some commercial and industrial assignments.

Call on advertising agencies in your area with your portfolio, and ask the art director to take a look at your work. It's a good idea to call ahead for an appointment, as art directors are usually pretty busy people. You'll find a list of advertising and public relations firms in the Yellow Pages.

You'll also want to show your portfolio to art and fashion directors of department stores and boutiques. Don't be bashful about requesting an appointment to show your work; never apologize for taking up their time. You're selling a service they need, and they're always on the lookout for a photographer who produces quality work.

Business and industrial firms should also have the opportunity to see your portfolio. Ask for an appointment with the public relations director or director of communications. Always be prepared to discuss ways in which his firm can use your services. Suggest possibilities and ask for his suggestions. If you have a sincere desire to help him do his job and make him look good by providing quality photographs, it will always come through in the discussion. He'll remember not only your work, but the interest you expressed in working with him.

Show your portfolio to anybody who will look at it; you never know who'll be the next person to need a photograph. Carry it around in your car all the time. Let your family take it to the hairdresser and the pool hall and show it to all the people they visit with.

Do work that makes you proud, and then don't hesitate to show it off every chance you get. You don't necessarily have to pat yourself on the back, but if you don't, who will?

County and State Fairs

Many county fairs and most state fairs have photography contests, right along with the sewing, baking, canning, etc. Even if you don't win, you'll have your work displayed, and thousands of people may look at it.

A popular game at fairs is finding reasons why the judges were wrong. Fairgoers always pick out their favorites, and they don't often agree with the judges. Not winning might be in your favor! But if you do win, you get a ribbon and usually a cash prize.

Most of these contests are divided into two divisions: amateur and professional. Most professionals don't take the time or effort to enter. You should! Never miss an opportunity to show your work in a place where many people may see it. And if you win, remember that the weekly newspaper will probably run a story and carry the winning photo—if you write it up and take it to them (see Chapter 6 for more weekly newspaper opportunities).

Other Contests

Photo contests abound. You'll find them on the local, state, and national levels. Many company newsletters have an annual contest which is open only to employees. Local and statewide newspapers have contests from time to time, as do statewide and regional magazines. There are national contests sponsored by pet food companies, shampoo and beauty product companies, baby food companies, and so on. Photography magazines also sponsor contests for their readers.

Whether or not it's worth your time to enter such events is a decision you'll have to make. I've entered many local and statewide contests and won several. I feel these are worthwhile because the competition is far less than you find in national contests. Your chances of winning are better, and even though you won't get the amount of publicity in a local contest that you would in a national one, the publicity will

This shot was originally set up to demonstrate the hairpiece, but I have used it in a promotional brochure, in exhibits of my work, and in a slide show selling my photographic services. I've booked several portraits of young women who wanted to be posed like this model. Get all the mileage you can out of a good photograph. Remember, you're acting wise when you advertise.

reach local people who are potential customers.

If you do decide to enter a photo contest, take the time to study the entry blank and the rules. Know what you may be giving up for the chance to win a prize. Some contests have a provision on their entry forms that your entry (or, in some cases, only the winning entry) becomes the property of the sponsor. In that case, once you sign the entry and send it off, you may have lost that photograph forever. You might want to avoid any contest that has such a stipulation.

Business Cards

Business cards are a natural. Leave some in the office of your local newspaper, and always carry an ample supply with you. Purchased in quantity, a good grade of business card can be had for less than a penny a card. And you never know when that penny card will bring you a hundred-dollar assignment!

Believe it or not, I've known a great many people who invest in business cards and then leave them in a box sitting in a desk drawer at home. Pass 'em out, man! Sprinkle the neighborhood with those little cards! I'll give you a couple of examples.

I got a call one afternoon from a man who owned a local industrial plant. He was walking down the sidewalk of the local shopping center and spotted one of my business cards lying on the pavement. Out of curiosity, he picked it up and read it. It just so happened that he'd been at a real estate office in the shopping center, where he was negotiating for a piece of property adjacent to his plant, and he needed aerial photographs of the property for the bank loan and several other uses. I got the job—and a nice one at that.

(Mind you, I'm not advocating littering with your business cards. I don't know who threw that card on the sidewalk, but whoever it was sure did me a favor!)

The drugstore and soda fountain that I frequent for coffee breaks has a little community bulletin board used for lost-and-found and for-sale items. This board happens to be near the greeting card, shower invitation, and gift wrap racks. I know of at least five weddings that I've booked over the years by keeping a business card posted on this board.

I also make it a practice to attach a business card to every letter, bill, and photographic order I send out.

Word of Mouth

This little phrase represents the best kind of advertising you can possibly have. You can't buy it and you can't ask for it. Word of mouth advertising comes only from satisfied customers who are pleased with the quality of your work, the dependability and sincere interest you show in fulfilling their needs, and the promptness with which you deliver their orders. Word of mouth is the only kind of advertising that has to be deserved. When your work and your reputation reach that point, it will come automatically.

Chapter Six

Crack the Weekly Newspaper Market

(You don't have to be a journalist)

Becoming associated with a weekly newspaper was the best move I ever made as a freelance photographer. That's how I got my start, as a teenager in my hometown. Years later, when I settled down after college and the service, I began my career at a newspaper in my adopted town.

Weekly newspapers have been the training ground for many reporters and photographers who've gone on to greater triumphs. They can also be a source of profitable contacts for the person who doesn't aspire to greatness, but just wants to make a good living freelancing.

There aren't many towns in this country too small to have a weekly. I've known some of these newspapers to have a circulation as small as five hundred, but they still publish every week and serve their community.

In the past, cities large enough to support one or more daily newspapers usually didn't have a weekly; they were for the small, country towns. But the trend now is for a larger city to be ringed with "bedroom communities" whose smaller publications concentrate more on community news that the large daily papers can't afford the space to report.

It's not unusual for one publisher to own several weekly newspapers. These may all be in the vicinity of one large city, or spread out across the entire state. I knew of one publisher who owned more than twenty different weekly newspapers. While each of these had a local office in the town it served, the local staffs were very small. All of the typesetting, layout, and printing was done at the headquarters location. This publisher provided a lucrative market for a freelancer who traveled the entire state. Just about every town he passed through was a source of photographs for one of these weekly newspapers.

It's in these community newspapers that the freelance photographer has access to some of his best customers. Weeklies are family publications. They cover local citizens from birth to death and everything in between—dance school recitals, Little League ball teams, school activities, graduations, engagements, marriages, business successes and promotions. And in each of these milestones of life, there's a job possibility for the freelance photographer.

Small Advertisers—Potential Customers

Most advertisers in weekly newspapers are small businesses— small businesses that need photographs from time to time. Every one of them is a potential customer.

Exposure (no pun intended) is the key to success for the freelance photographer. There's no better exposure or advertising possible than to be in close contact with the subscribers and advertisers of a weekly newspaper. You get to meet them personally while on assignments for the publication. Through your credit line on photographs published in the newspaper, they quickly become familiar with your name and with the quality and diversity of your work.

Most weeklies have a very small staff made up of versatile individuals who can—and do—handle more than one job. Seldom do you find anyone who is strictly a reporter, photographer, or editor. Even if the publication has a full-time photographer, chances are he can't cover everything that needs to be covered.

Getting Started

Take high school athletics, for instance. There are few weekly newspapers whose circulation area doesn't include more than one high school. Helping out with coverage on sports when both teams are playing in town at the same time is a good way to break in with a paper.

Maybe you won't get a lot of work at first, but all it takes is one or two assignments to show the editor or publisher the quality of your photographs, and you'll be on your way. Shoot some assignments on speculation, and then take them to the editor and ask if the paper can use them. If you should ever happen on the scene of a wreck or fire, these are potential sure sellers.

Are you a member of a local civic club that's about to elect officers, or award a scholarship to a student, or present some books to the library, or erect a sign at the edge of town? Photograph these activities. Weekly newspapers love to publicize such events.

Does your church have a new pastor or choir director? Do the Girl or Boy Scout troops it sponsors have an unusual project? Are you having a special guest speaker next Sunday? Weekly newspapers love church-related activities.

What about your local garden club? Did they just have a club competition and present winning contestants with ribbons? Are they beautifying the local park or the entrance to a subdivision by planting flowers or trees? Did they take some arrangements to a nursing home or hospital?

Did your neighbor catch a lunker bass? Did your doctor just break the course record at the country club? Did your son just win the tennis championship? Did your daughter's teacher just come back from a trip to Mexico, loaded down with souvenirs?

Did you get caught speeding by the radar gun the local police department just purchased? They're proud of that new unit, and selling that photo could help pay for your speeding ticket.

Now, granted, none of these are earthshaking news events, but they're the kind of photos you see in weekly newspapers all the time. The reason you see them is that someone spent the time to shoot the photographs, and that weekly newspapers love to run photos of local people.

Weekly newspapers also, at times, get carried away with human interest photographs and animal photographs. If you should happen to see a horse nibbling away at an apple that's still in the tree, or a dog kissing a youngster smack-dab on the mouth, or a rabbit and a cat playing with each other, or children playing in a mud puddle or under a garden hose—you've probably got yourself a salable photograph.

Photographs shot on speculation are a good way to get started with your weekly newspaper. It won't cost you much money or time to shoot a few photos like the ones I've talked about, and it could be a great beginning!

For the editor of a weekly newspaper, finding a part-time photographer who's dependable and who can take a decent photograph is like the answer to a prayer. If he discovers that you have those two qualities—especially always showing up where and when you're supposed to—you'll be on the road to a long-lasting relationship.

Now, don't expect to get rich off assignments from a weekly newspaper. You'll receive a *nominal* fee for each photograph published. If you're lucky, you can haggle for some photo supplies every now and then and even some mileage for the use of your car. But the real value of this working agreement, as stated earlier, is in the contacts you'll make— the potential customers you'll be able to meet and impress.

More Than a Photo

If you're going to be selling photographs to the newspaper, you've got to give them more than a photo. What good is a picture of an auto

This picture story was shot for a weekly newspaper to depict a summer weekend at a local lake. It is typical of the photojournalism assignments you can expect from a local newspaper.

accident if you don't know who was involved in it? How interesting is a picture of a fire if you don't know where or how it happened, or whether the building was destroyed?

The information under a photograph in a publication is the *cutline.* If the photograph is run in conjunction with an article, then the information in the cutline may be very brief. If the photograph is run alone, the cutline must contain all the information needed to support the photograph.

Some photographers are also adequate, even excellent, writers. Some can't put five words together on paper and have them make sense. The important thing is that you get the information to go along with your photograph. If you can put it into readable form, fine. If not, just provide the "raw" information for the newspaper and let them write it the way they want.

Many times a photographer will shoot a picture and leave the scene immediately in his haste to get it developed and see how great it is. Don't! By far the easiest time to get the information is right there and then, while all the participants are still on the scene, not the next day or "next week." Don't put off getting your information if you expect to sell the photograph.

Credit Lines

You should be sure to reach an agreement with the editor right from the beginning about receiving a credit line ("Photo by _____") on each of your photographs, in type big enough to be seen easily by the reader.

You'll be photographing a lot of different children, and people are proud of their children and their accomplishments. They're also proud of the photographer who did such an excellent job for the newspaper. Every credit line is a free advertisement!

Advertising for Yourself

You might also be able to work out a trade-off and receive a certain amount of space in each issue, or every other issue, to advertise your photography. With this arrangement, you're taking a part of your fee in advertising. Mention this possibility, especially if the editor says he can't offer you much money at the start. Such an arrangement can really be helpful if you're just getting your freelance business established.

An ad doesn't have to be big to attract reader interest. A small advertisement with an eye-catching design can be quite effective. You're a photographer; do a job for yourself! *Assignment:* a storytelling photograph that will sell your services to the reader.

Information Please

You'd be surprised at how many people use the offices of a weekly newspaper as an information bureau. Readers are constantly calling in asking for advice about businesses in the area, including photographers. If you're doing work for a weekly, it's only natural that for any photographic inquiries the staff will be more than willing to give people your name, if they know you're interested in the work.

Make certain that everyone in the office knows you're a freelancer, and knows how to get in touch with you. It's also a good idea to leave some copies of your price list (if you've developed one) in the office, as well as a listing of the types of work you can handle—passport photos, outdoor portraits, aerials, commercial and industrial shots, etc.

By the way, most weekly newspapers also sell business cards, rubber stamps, and bill- and letterheads. As a staffer, you'll surely get a discount. You might even get the wholesale price, which is usually 50 percent of list!

Engagement Photos

Most young women who are planning a wedding will have their engagement photos published in the weekly newspaper several months in advance. Many times they'll ask the newspaper if they have a photographer who'll take this engagement photo for them.

Have you developed that nose for freelance business yet? A woman interested in an engagement photo for a newspaper is the best prospect for a wedding order you could hope for!

Even if you don't shoot the engagement portrait, by working for a newspaper you'll have first access to the news of just about every potential bride in the neighborhood. Many studios that specialize in wedding photography immediately call or mail a brochure to every woman whose engagement announcement appears in a newspaper. You'll have at least a day's jump on them to make your phone call or send out your brochure.

See what I mean? The potential customers you can meet, as well as other advantages of working with a weekly newspaper, are almost unending!

Chapter Seven

Wedding Photography

(Here comes the bride, with her checkbook)

There'll always be weddings that need photographing, by studios, by freelancers, or by amateurs who have no idea what they're doing.

I've talked to many brides about doing their weddings, only to find out later that they decided to let Uncle Jasper or Cousin Walpole handle it. Now sometimes an uncle or cousin might be a pro—I photographed my niece's wedding—but usually they're rank amateurs who just bought themselves a "good camera" that takes "real good pictures."

I learned a long time ago not to argue with the bride who's made such a decision. Simply say "Thanks for your time," and go out in search of another prospect.

Where Do You Get Wedding Bookings?

Word of mouth advertising is usually the best in any field, but especially in the wedding business. If a bride is happy with her album, you can bet everybody who comes within a city block of her will be invited to "look at my beautiful wedding photographs."

I've done some newspaper advertising for weddings, but most of my work has come from referrals. I've made it a point to visit all the bridal shops, department stores, boutiques, florists, caterers who have a lot of wedding business, and especially printers to show my samples and ask for their help in booking weddings. Naturally I reciprocate by sending business their way whenever I get the chance.

Have a Contract

A contract is best for the protection of both the photographer and the bride so there won't be any misunderstandings. Make certain it states the time and location of the ceremony, the date, the picture order, exactly what the photographer is to deliver, the location of the reception, the bride's maiden name, what her married name will be, both her present and future addresses and telephone numbers, the name of the groom, and all parents' names (you don't want to get to the wedding and have to refer to everybody as "hey, you!").

Some photographers even go so far as to have a list of photo possibilities printed on the contract so that the bride can check off the ones she wants. If you follow such a list, there'll be no question as to whether you provided the coverage for which you contracted.

Some contracts contain a *release paragraph* stating that the photographer isn't responsible for loss of photographs through camera malfunction, accidents at the lab, loss of film in the mail, etc.

As stated in Chapter 5, some contracts also contain an advertising or model release giving the photographer the right to use any photos as samples or for advertising.

Setting the Fee. One of the most important details that should be covered in the contract is the fee. Make certain you have a complete understanding with the bride on exactly what you will charge for the work you intend to do.

There are many different ways to price weddings. Some photographers offer a complete package that includes engagement photograph for the newspaper, formal bridal portrait, and coverage of the rehearsal party, wedding, and reception. Others price the bridal portrait separately and then offer the balance in a package deal.

One of the best packages I ever offered of the wedding itself consisted of three albums: an 8x10 album for the bride and a 4x5 album for each set of parents (which I'll cover later in this chapter).

Weddings are among the most lucrative jobs you can get. It is not uncommon for a complete package, including the bridal portrait, to be in the $500 range. Many photographers have a $300 minimum charge for weddings.

You can see that only two or three weddings a month could easily earn you $10,000 per year, even if you didn't do anything else!

Get copies of several different contracts and pick the best features from each, or have your lawyer draw one up for you. You'll find pads of wedding contracts (just like the pads of model-release blanks) advertised in many photography magazines and sold in some larger camera stores.

What About the Amateurs?

Some contracts go so far as to state that "the photographer contracted for shall be the sole photographer taking photographs at the wedding." This can be used to bar relatives or friends who bring their Instamatics along and go about happily popping flashcubes in everybody's face, including yours.

I never like to go quite this far. But I've made a request at each wedding (and enforced it) that nobody else shoot until I got through with a pose. You should, however, explain to the bride that if you have to pose the group, take your photographs, and then wait for everybody else to take theirs before you can set up the next shot, considerable time will be added to the photographic process, and guests will be kept waiting in line at the reception.

You'd be amazed at how these amateurs take wedding shots. On several occasions I've seen them stand up in their seats when the bride entered the church and shoot away. I've actually seen them go up on the altar during the ceremony and lie on the floor between the clergyman and the bride and groom and shoot up at them—with flash!

Most ministers have rather strict rules about photos being taken with flash in the church during the ceremony. Even if they allowed it, I'd never want to interrupt the proceedings with a flash. I've always made it a point to tell the minister before the wedding that if he saw a flash go off during the ceremony, *it would not be mine.* I also ask permission to shoot with available light from the back of the church or the balcony.

Camera and Other Equipment

I always use a 2¼ camera, never a 35mm, for weddings. As stated before, there's a great difference in quality between the enlarged, finished prints of the former and those of the latter—especially on large group shots like the entire wedding party. On many weddings I've been able to sell prints up to 16x20 and 20x24 from candid negatives. I'd really be in a pickle if somebody wanted that 20x24 and I had used 35mm.

I like people to compare my wedding photographs to those shot at the ceremony by friends, whether the friend was using a 35mm, 126, or 110. The comparisons always help me to book additional weddings!

Other than your camera, you'll need a strobe for your light source and a tripod for your time exposures made during the ceremony. A shutter-release cable is also helpful.

What Scenes to Shoot

Listed here are the standard shots that I take at every wedding. There are, of course, many other potential shots, including unlimited possibilities for candids before and after the actual ceremony and at the reception.

The formal bridal portrait is usually part of the wedding package.
(Some freelance photographers
shoot only candid wedding shots
and let studios handle the formal
portraits.)

A happy bride and groom
almost always make for easy
shooting. I generally pose a shot
like this at the altar, and then
concentrate strictly on candid
shots during the reception.

Before the Ceremony

Bride with mother
Bride with both parents
Bride with ring bearer and flower girl
Bride with maid or matron of honor looking at her bouquet
Groom being congratulated by best man
Bride's mother ready to enter church on arm of usher
Groom's mother ready to enter church on arm of usher
Bride and father (or whoever is giving her away) just before
    they enter the church
Bride and father as they walk down the aisle (shot from the
    rear)

During the Ceremony

Several available-light shots either from the rear of sanctuary
    or the balcony
Bride and groom walking up the aisle

In the Sanctuary after the Ceremony
      Bride and groom at the altar
      Bride and groom at the altar with the minister
      Bride and groom with bridesmaids and flower girl
      Bride and groom with ushers, best man, father of bride, and
         ring bearer
      Bride and groom with entire wedding party
      Bride and groom with bride's family
      Bride and groom with groom's family
      Bride and groom with grandparents
      Bride and groom with musicians and soloists
      Bride and groom with other special relatives or friends
      Bride and groom kissing
      Close-up of bride's and groom's hands (rings showing) on
         Bible or bridal bouquet

At the Reception
      Bride and groom receiving guests
      Person in charge of the guest book
      Persons helping serve
      Various shots of the receiving line
      Bride and groom cutting cake
      Bride feeding groom a piece of cake
      Groom feeding bride a piece of cake
      Bride and groom toasting
      Candid shots of bride and groom visiting with friends, eating,
         kissing, etc.
      Bride and groom signing marriage license
      Groom removing bride's garter
      Groom throwing garter to ushers
      Mother helping bride remove corsage from bouquet
      Bride throwing bouquet to bridesmaids
      People decorating car
      Bride and groom in their going-away outfits
      Bride and groom leaving in a hail of rice
      Bride and groom in the decorated car

There are hundreds more that you can shoot, including some special effects (double exposures, couple's faces lighted by candles, etc.); however, I never push these unless the bride requests them.

To Proof or Not to Proof

There are two ways you can handle the order once you've finished shooting: You can have proofs made up of all shots and let the bride and parents order from the proofs, or you can have everything printed up in the size the bride wants her album, usually 5x7 or 8x10.

I've done both. It's more expensive to have proofs made and then have finished prints made, but sometimes you can sell the proof album in addition to the finished album. You can buy a 4x5 proof album that has an order blank opposite each page so that the clients can check off the size and number of prints to be made from each proof. It's very simple to remove these order pages, and then you have a finished 4x5 wedding album.

If you have everything printed to size ("process and print" orders), you'll pay less for the finished prints, but you might not be able to sell all of them. When I've gone this route, and the bride picked out the prints for her album and then indicated those were all she wanted, I've offered her all the remaining prints at a much lower price, usually enough to cover all my expenses on the wedding. More often than not, I've been taken up on such an offer.

When you "process and print," you'll have to let the families make up their order from the bride's finished album. Usually I number my negatives in the order that prints are placed in the album. This simplifies reorders quite a bit, but be sure to ask the bride not to change the sequence of the photographs until everyone has placed an order.

A Great Package Deal. Some labs offer a special deal on "process and print" orders that includes one 8x10 and two 4x5s of each negative, sort of like a giant prom set. You can get these at the terrific prices offered only if you order the "wedding combo package" (or whatever name they call it at different labs) when you send in the film to be processed. You can't get this package deal on prints from already processed negatives. By ordering this special offer, you can give the bride an 8x10 album for herself, and a 4x5 album for each set of parents. It's a great little money-maker!

Collecting Your Money

I can't emphasize this too strongly: *Always* collect your money—or the majority of it—before the wedding! Some photographers don't, and far too many times they end up having to wait a long time to collect their payments.

I've never understood why a photographer should feel hesitant about asking for his money in advance. Everybody else does—the dress shop, the printer, the caterer, the florist—everybody but the preacher, and he always gets his.

Young couples don't want to gyp you out of your money, but in most cases after the wedding, the honeymoon, and the cost of getting some type of household established, money is usually a little scarce. They can wait for their album; they know the photographer isn't going to throw it in the trash because he hasn't been paid. They know he'll be more than willing to hand it over when they eventually get the money, although it may take six months or a year. They never stop to think that the photographer has bills to pay, too.

So get your money before you shoot, even from friends and relatives. *Especially* from friends and relatives!

Questions of Protocol

You may feel uneasy asking this, but it's important for you to know if there will be any divorced parents involved in the wedding. Don't depend on the bride to tell you; she may not think to mention it. If there are, find out exactly who the bride wants to include in the family group photos. Should both divorced parents be included in the same photo with the bride and groom, or should there be separate photos for each parent? If the divorced parents have remarried, should their spouses also be in the photo? If you know just what the situation is and just what the bride wants, you can control the procedure and prevent some embarrassing moments at the wedding for everybody, including yourself.

At country or small-town weddings, you can also ask if anybody chews tobacco. If so, put them at the end of the line near a potted plant or fern. The same goes for snuff-dippers.

Little Helpers

At *every* wedding you'll run into them. "Quick, get that shot of Aunt Mira drinking champagne. She never drinks champagne. They'll surely want a shot of that."

The Little Helpers are well-meaning friends or relatives, each one an expert on wedding photography. Little Helpers will try to pull you away just as the bride is getting ready to cut the cake. "I know they'll want this picture. My little daughter is eating out of the rice bowl." The *"they"* to which Little Helpers refer are people I've never been able to identify. Certainly they're not the bride and groom.

If you shot every photograph you were ordered to shoot at a wedding, it would take a truck to haul the film away. So many of the things they see that are "so cute and would make excellent pictures for the album" involve their children—scooping up handfuls of wedding cake and throwing it at a cousin, drinking directly out of the punch bowl, eating the flowers in the table arrangement.

I always try not to be rude. The best thing is to thank them for the suggestion, but tell them you're busy right now. Sometimes I tell them that I just took that shot, or that I'm running out of film and am afraid I'll have to pass that one up.

Just remember, the bride and her parents are paying the bill. Take your orders from them. I've yet to find a Little Helper who was willing to pay for a photograph he or she ordered you to shoot.

Not Always in Church

All weddings don't take place in churches. I've photographed them in homes (large and small), in apartments (small and smaller), in gardens, by the side of a lake, at a motel. I even know of one that was held on a flatbed truck in the middle of a shopping center parking lot. I didn't photograph that one, however; my daughter did.

Weather, of course, is the only bad part about outdoor weddings (well, not the only bad part; there are also bugs and dogs, gopher holes to step in, and other problems). One thing you can count on: The wind will always blow. Not much you can do about it. Just be patient and wait for a chance to shoot the bride when her dress isn't caught up in a gust.

Brides seem also to like to get married in the dark for some reason—by candlelight or in as dim a place as possible. After the ceremony, you'll have to ask someone to turn on enough lights so you can see to focus. For available-light shots during the ceremony, I focus on the lighted candles.

Don't count on people involved with the wedding to have any consideration whatsoever when it comes to arranging things for the benefit of the photographer. It just won't happen. People will walk up to the bride and groom at the reception and start talking, or hug them, even though they see you standing there with your camera trained on the couple and your strobe held aloft, ready to shoot.

I photographed one wedding at a home in the country where they put the archway under which the bride and groom were to be married right in front of an old tool shed. I believe that's the only wedding I ever photographed where the background consisted of rotted wood and a rusted tin roof. There was also a plow in a lot of the pictures.

Another time at an outdoor wedding, the barbecue caterer parked his delivery truck right behind the altar. I had to start it up and drive it out of the way. Somehow I didn't think it appropriate to have a pig on a spit, complete with an apple in his mouth, hovering between the bride and groom and the minister, to be remembered ever after. If you can change a bad background, change it. If not, you'll just have to make the best of the situation.

Be Prepared

Don't expect to go to a wedding and just shoot photographs! Maybe some of the elite studios can do this, but I'm always called on to help out in any rough situation. It just doesn't seem polite to turn down those anguished pleas for help when people are obviously in desperate straits. Some of the things I've been called on to do include: helping the minister find the marriage license (which had been misplaced in his cluttered office), and searching the church to find out where the florist left the bridal bouquet and the flowers for the bridesmaids. (One time he left them at another church!)

There was one time when the florist got the dates mixed up and didn't bring any flowers to the church. Who do you think ran outside, picked some flowers, and bunched them together into a bouquet with masking tape?

There was another time when the wedding director forgot to come. Who do you think directed the wedding?

There's no such thing as a dull wedding! Something always goes wrong, and you never know what's going to happen next. The only thing you can count on is the "I do"—and there are some where the "I do" never does. Yep, I've even had one of those—two, as a matter of fact.

Chapter Eight

The Dance School Gold Mine

(Would you like to earn $3,000 from one job?)

As a photographer, you'll be interested in dance schools only once a year, when recital time rolls around. Who can resist beautiful color photos of those little dolls in their costumes? It's a chance for you to make good money and make a lot of people happy at the same time.

Dance schools are everywhere; they've really gotten to be big business. Some dance school owners in larger cities rent space once a week to hold classes in even the smallest towns or rural areas. Community centers are a favorite meeting place, and I've even known of dance classes held in warehouses.

Dance schools are probably the biggest single jobs that you could ever hope to get. I believe the smallest amount I ever made from a dance school assignment was $500, and that was a very small school. If there are any dance schools in your area, you should make them your first target. They're money-makers of the highest order.

I photographed one dance school for more than eleven years. I worked less than three full days out of the year on this one account and usually cleared at least $3,000. This particular school averaged an enrollment of approximately five hundred students. While I also worked with other, smaller dance schools, this one always had priority on choice of dates since it was my first, as well as my largest.

Best Working Method

Over the years, the owner of the school and I tried several different methods to find the most efficient manner to do the photographs, as well as to produce the most sales.

The idea is to offer both individual photos of the students, as well as class group photos. I provided the school with a free 5x7 color photograph of each class, and there were around fifty classes. I would also throw in some action shots of some of the best students, for the school to use in its advertising campaign for the following year.

At the start, I tried to do the work at dress rehearsals. I would photograph each class as they came on stage for their dance. The recital was held in a high school that had a large auditorium. I had a setup in a hall just off the stage where I would rush after each group to make individual photos. This method didn't work very well with a large school, but I have since used it with much smaller schools. With the large school there was always a lot of confusion, especially with the younger students, and the pace was just too hectic. Even though they spread dress rehearsal out over two afternoons and two nights, there wasn't enough time to do the job properly.

One of the agreements I had with each dance school was that the director of the school or one of the teachers would pose each child for me, to insure authentic stances and make the students look as professional as possible. With everyone concentrating on rehearsal, it left very little time for posing.

I finally decided I would set up at the dance school for an entire week before the recital. Then I would photograph each class at their regularly scheduled class time. This would give the school and parents an opportunity to check on costumes to make sure everybody had all the pieces, and that everything fit, before the actual recital. It also gave the students the chance to go through their dance routines in costumes one time before dress rehearsal.

This particular school usually had three classes scheduled during the same time period, which was no problem at all. I would bring one class at a time into the room that I'd set up for photographs. Individual photos were made of each student who wanted them; then the entire group was assembled for the class group photo.

As mentioned earlier, each teacher or the director was responsible for posing each individual who wanted a photograph and for posing the class group. When the photographer doesn't have to worry about posing, it removes a lot of responsibility and worry, allowing him to concentrate entirely on making a good photograph.

Because I scheduled the photographs over a five-day period, usually between the hours of 3 p.m. and 5 or 6 p.m., neither I nor the students were rushed. Another important advantage was that mothers had an opportunity to visit with each other in the waiting room and talk about how pretty the costumes were and who they sent the dance photos to. In other words, the mothers helped drum up business for me with these conversations while I was busy shooting photographs.

I always made it a point to display in the waiting room some of the better photos from the previous year. The school always displayed all the class group photos, changing their display every year. In the waiting room there was also a professionally printed poster, which explained the cost of the two types of photos available.

No Mothers Allowed!

One important point: Mothers of the students weren't allowed in the camera room while I was photographing, only the students themselves. I always found that the children were much more self-conscious when their parents or a brother or sister was watching them be photographed.

The director and I pointed out to the parents that by enforcing this rule we could give them much better photographs of their children. While there were some complaints, no exceptions were made. Most parents understood and were willing to cooperate. In more than eleven years, I recall only one case in which a child cried—because her mother was outside—so that we couldn't take her picture. And then the mother brought her back the next day and everything went smoothly.

This is another advantage of spreading the session out over the week: Children who are absent from their regular class can always come back another day to have their individual photos taken, even though they have missed the class group photo.

What Photos to Offer

While there are many different photo packages you can offer, I settled quite early on a standard "prom set" and never varied. All the photos were in color. For individual student photos, the package consisted of two 5x7s and four wallet photos. For class group photos, there was one 5x7 of the entire class.

There were several reasons for this decision. First, the package of two 5x7s and four wallets is the old standby prom package, which almost all labs offer. With more than twenty-four or thirty negatives in the order, you usually get a price break from the lab. These packages are very economical.

Such orders at the lab are machine processed and printed, which means that everything you send in is printed, and you pay for every exposure. Some labs will edit for you and not print obviously bad shots; others will not.

Some photographers offer packages that include 8x10s or more wallet photos, but I didn't. I always wanted to keep the price of the initial package as low as I could and still make good money on it.

Also, I always counted on making some money on reprint orders. I always placed a price list in each package, which gave the reprint charges. In many cases parents would order as many as a dozen extra wallet photos after they'd seen the finished prints. I've also had them

What parent could resist a photo of a little doll like this? That's one reason dance schools can be a number one producer on your quest for $25,000 a year from your freelance photography.

order reprints from 8x10s to 20x24s on a regular basis. Naturally you can afford to charge more for reprint orders, and you'll probably want to go to something better than machine processing for your reprints.

One reason I chose the 5x7 size for the class groups was that I like to shoot such photographs with my 35mm camera, and I don't like to offer anything larger than a 5x7 from a 35mm negative. Also, most dance schools don't have the room to display 8x10 prints of every class if they're large enough to have fifty or sixty classes. The display of these group photos during the course of the year always helped increase my sales at recital time.

The class group photo is really a secondary offer, primarily for parents who feel they can't afford individual photos but still want the child to be able to buy something. However, many of them always wanted the group as well as the individual photos.

I've worked with smaller schools that did want 8x10 group photos, in which case I went to a 120 film size and, naturally, charged more.

One Pose per Student

This is the rule I've always followed. If a student wanted more than one pose in the same costume, or in a different costume, each pose constituted a different package. I found that in some schools there were students who might be in as many as six or seven different dances in the recital, and they wanted a photograph in each costume.

How many shots do you shoot of each student? This is something you'll have to work out for yourself. I always made only one shot per student. By watching the viewfinder closely and by waiting for just the right expression, I could tell at the time of the shot if I had a good photograph. With practice and concentration, you can tell if the subject blinks at the moment the shutter is tripped. In the event they do close their eyes, laugh, wet on the roll-paper background, etc. (and I've had all these happen), then you have to go ahead and make another exposure.

If you have a lab that will edit your shots and not charge you for every exposure, if you've included the extra cost of film and processing, and if you're not sure you can tell whether you've got a good shot or not—then you might want to go ahead and make several shots of each student.

The very few times that customers complained about not having a choice of poses, I'd point out that the prices they were paying for these packages were so low that showing them proofs was out of the question. I was always able to quote them the prices on a regular portrait session that would include much more of the photographer's time and a wide variety of proofs for selection. Since there was such a vast difference in price (even considering the fact that my portrait prices were always reasonable), they quickly understood the reason for having only one shot per pose.

Prom Set Masks

As mentioned previously, these photos are machine printed, and each lab has a specific size of printing mask for them. The mask covers all but a specific area of the negative, and that's all of the negative that's included in the photo. There are no exceptions.

A mask may be something like one and five-eighths by one and seven-eighths inches for 120 film, but it does vary from lab to lab, depending on which make of machine printer they use.

Be sure to know the mask size before you start shooting. That is, *before* you have a whole bunch of photos with people's heads, feet, or arms cut off! Cut a mask out of cardboard in the same proportions as the one the printer will use, and drop it in your viewfinder.

Labs will also use a mask for your group photos. Usually the lab will include a page of the various masks they use in the brochure or booklet that outlines their prices and services. If it isn't in the book, the lab will have the masks available on a separate sheet. Be sure to ask for one. Some labs will also provide a mask to fit in the viewfinder of your camera, but you'll have to ask.

How to Collect Your Money

You'll recall I mentioned earlier that we made individual photos of every student *who wanted them.* It's most important that you receive your money before the photographs are made! You'd be surprised at how hard it is to collect if you wait until you make delivery.

Many families move out of town after the school year; others get mad with the dance school for some reason. Some will have taken their own photos at the recital and then decided they don't want yours no matter how good they are. And then there are just the plain old deadbeats, who seem to take great delight in trying to beat a photographer out of the money due him.

This is the one rule to which there should be absolutely no exceptions! All literature and posters should state: *Orders must be paid for at the time photographs are made.*

Getting the Word Out

When I worked with dance schools, mimeographed forms were prepared by the school and sent home to each family, explaining the procedure for the photographic sessions, the costs, how the photos would be delivered, etc. Half of the form consisted of an order blank, which the child was to bring, together with payment, to the class on the day photos were to be taken.

The school usually found that the best way to be sure the forms were taken home was to put them in the plastic bags that contained the recital costumes. There were always additional forms at the reception desk for those who forgot to bring them back.

Delivery of Photos

Since photos are taken near the end of the dance school year, delivery can pose a problem. I solved this by using two different methods, and both worked.

First, the order form announced several pick-up dates on which parents could stop by the dance school to get their orders. These were usually scheduled at least a month after the photos were taken to insure adequate time to get the orders back from the lab, identify them, and package them.

The second manner of distribution was by mail. Although this is somewhat more troublesome, it does cut down on phone calls from parents who forget the pick-up dates and want you to make other arrangements for them to get their pictures. When mailing orders, I always added an extra charge to cover envelopes and postage.

The teachers or the director always helped to identify the photographs. As a backup, each order form was numbered with a roll and frame number at the time the photo was taken, but it's much easier to have teachers do the identification because they know all the students by sight. This is especially important when mailing.

Equipment and Setup

I always used a Mamiya C330 for the individual student photos. The lens was the 80mm normal. Lighting was accomplished with one strobe bounced out of an umbrella, high and directly behind the camera. This gives a broad, somewhat flat type of lighting, but it works quite adequately, considering the range in the size of the students, the flashiness of their costumes, and the variety of poses.

Group shots were made with a 35mm camera, a normal lens, and a hand-held strobe.

Background for the individual shots was roll paper, with one roll usually being adequate for a five-hundred-student school. The paper was supported by two heavy-duty light stands with a ten-foot closet pole (one and a half inches in diameter) suspended between them and run through the roll of paper. A hole was drilled through each end of the pole so it would fit atop the light stands.

Another way to build a support for the paper is to use a nine-and-a-half-foot piece of half-inch galvanized pipe with elbow joints on each end. Put the pipe through the roll of paper and insert the ends of your light stands into the elbow joints.

If you ever bend or crease a roll of background paper, you might just as well throw it away. There's nothing you can do to keep the wrinkles from showing up in your photographs. A good way to carry these nine-foot rolls around and give them some protection is to get a long piece of five-inch-diameter plastic sewer pipe with caps on both ends. This paper can then be tied atop your car on the luggage rack.

My entire equipment list for a dance school job consisted of:

Two cameras: one 2¼x2¼; one 35mm
One umbrella
Two strobes
One tripod
Three light stands
One roll-paper background
Support for roll of paper
One extension sync cord
One roll of masking tape

Approaching the School

Dance schools depend on repeat business; therefore, they're most interested in dealing only with photographers who can offer professional services to their students. Many of the schools with which I've worked had bad experiences with other photographers in the form of poor photographs, long-delayed deliveries, and in some cases no deliveries at all and no refund of the money. In approaching a school, be prepared to show them quality samples. Point out that you're local and that you also have a reputation to uphold. Explain to them that they're offering a real service to their students by providing your professional services, conveniently located at the school.

Be sure to point out to the director the importance of having the dance teachers do the posing to insure professional poses. This was always one important advantage I felt I had over other photographers who didn't insist on this. Too many times dance students just walk onto the paper background and stand there while the photographer snaps away. My photographs, even of the little children in the beginning classes, made students look like professional dancers because of the posing, the background, and the lighting—but especially the posing.

In terms of "what's in it for the school," some of them will want a commission on each package. If it's necessary in order for you to get the account, this really doesn't present any problem; just add it onto the price you were going to charge. None of my schools ever insisted on a commission, and I never mentioned it to them. I think they thought of photographs as a service to the students and were quite happy to receive a free photo of each class, plus any photos they needed for advertising. If the director or teachers had their own children taking lessons, I usually never charged for those individual photographs, and I always offered a free package to each teacher.

Many dancing school teachers are like a lot of real estate agents; once they've been with the firm a few years and seen all that money rolling in, they start entertaining thoughts of starting their own business. It never hurts to be extra nice to the dance teachers, because you never know when one of them might be pulling out to start her own school, and who do you think she'll call for photographs?

Added Benefit

If you're able to maintain a successful working relationship with a dance school over a period of years, it will also bring you quite a few additional assignments as students and parents become familiar with the quality of your work.

I've been called on to do many family group portraits through dance school contacts. At last count, I've done sixty weddings of beautiful young women whom I first photographed in their dance recital costumes. I've also been privileged to photograph some of their children!

Dance schools are truly a gold mine for the freelance photographer. These once-a-year accounts can lead to year-round business, if you handle them right and turn out quality work!

Chapter Nine

Children's Sports

(Pint-size pros)

The next time you go to a Little League baseball game—or a children's football, basketball, or soccer game—watch the action in the stands instead of on the field. I'll guarantee that after a little while you'll begin to wonder whether the games are staged for the benefit of the kids or the parents.

Regardless, children's sports offer another very profitable opportunity for the freelance photographer. At the beginning of the season, all teams want group shots as well as individual photos of each player. At the end of the season, it's time for group and individual photographs of the championship team, plus the all-star team for each league.

The amount of money you can earn from photographing children's sports depends on how many teams or how many leagues you're able to line up. There are usually at least ten teams in any kind of league. Depending on the sport, there will be anywhere from ten to thirty children on a team. It doesn't take much skill at multiplication to see that this can amount to a good income.

How to Make Contact

There are so many different organizations involved in children's sports now that it's hard to pick one approach and say it works best. There will be situations where you'll have to contact each individual coach and work out an arrangement with him. I've worked with some leagues that are actively run by a director, or a committee, who sets up photographic sessions with each team; therefore, I had to deal with only one person (or a small group), not with each coach.

There have been other times when my dealings in making arrangements for the photographs were primarily with the sponsors of the various teams. In some leagues business sponsors pay for everything. In church leagues you'll usually deal with one person at each church who can coordinate photographing all the teams. Leagues sponsored by the YWCA or YMCA will usually have one person who can set up a schedule for all teams.

A good way to find out what organizations are operating in your area is to contact the city or county recreation department. They'll probably be handling some leagues themselves and will know about others who are using their facilities.

Prom Sets Again

Many of the same procedures for photographing dance schools also apply to sports. First, try to make the subjects look as professional as possible. Coaches can help with posing, just as dance school teachers do. You'll have many more sales if you can make each youngster look like a scaled-down version of a real pro in his or her particular sport.

Even if your subject is a peewee, try to interpret him as well on film as if he were a big-name player. Such an attitude on your part will definitely show up in your finished work. Remember, there's more to a photograph than good lighting and being in focus.

In most cases with children's teams, I offer the standard package: two 5x7s and four wallets of the individual, plus a 5x7 or 8x10 group photo.

Some labs also offer various packages with such names as "Sports Mates" or "Memory Mates" or "Team Mates." These packages consist of various sizes; the most common is a 5x7 team group shot and a 3x5 photo of the individual player, mounted in a cardboard frame or mat and usually containing the name of the team and the year printed on it. These packages usually run a little more than the standard prom package, and they also give the individual fewer photos.

Children's sports photography is another situation in which you definitely want to collect your money in advance. Some coaches will cooperate by collecting the money for you; other times you'll have to take it on the spot just before you shoot each player.

Equipment, Lighting, and Setup

I prefer the 2¼ camera for the individual shots. If the group shot is a 5x7, I usually use my 35mm camera. If it's an 8x10, I'll switch to the 2¼ or the Mamiya Press, which gives me a 2¼x3¼ negative.

Lighting and setup for these sports photos is usually quite a bit less complicated than for a dance school. You're in the open with the playing field itself as your background in baseball, football, and soccer. If you're inside with basketball, ice hockey, or swimming, you don't have to worry about roll-paper backgrounds.

Individual photos like this, plus a group shot of the entire team, are what you'll usually shoot for children's teams. Simple poses work best in showing off the player and the uniform. Action poses usually mean trouble—arms covering the face, or pained expressions as the player concentrates on the action rather than the photograph.

Your biggest worry with backgrounds for sports is being certain you don't end up with a bunch of onlookers or other players in your field of view. Cluttered backgrounds only take away from your subject, and he's the one (or his parents) who's paying for the photograph, not fans in the stands or on the field.

Outdoors, the sun provides your lighting; just be careful of the shadows. Have the baseball player slide his cap back on his head a little so the bill doesn't throw his face into shadow. It's best to try to convince football players to hold the helmets in their arms or put them on the ground in front of them. Mom and Dad can't see much of their faces with those contraptions on their heads.

If the sun is harsh and you don't want the subjects looking directly into it (resulting in squinted eyes and screwed-up faces), consider having them turn away from the sun. Then use a flash fill so you can get faces lighted and not have them so dark that all you see are teeth and whites of eyes. Flash fill is most effective on very bright days.

Try to arrange your sessions so you're not shooting too late in the afternoon. Using flash in late afternoon will give you a black background as though it were night. If you don't use flash in the fading sunlight, you'll pick up a warm, orangish cast to skin tones, and your overall photo will be too warm. The coaches won't be aware of this; so be sure to tell them why you want to shoot in the morning or early afternoon.

On sports shots indoors, you'll probably want to use your umbrella to help cut down shadows.

Poses

You'll find that often your subject will want some dramatic pose, such as sliding into base, or diving through the air, or jumping off the ground to catch a ball. More often than not, if you go along with him, you'll end up with extended arms completely obscuring the face, a facial expression that looks like a fully puffed-up blowfish, or the impression that the subject is undergoing excruciating pain.

Stick with the standard poses such as a batter poised for a pitch, an infielder with one foot on the base ready to take a throw, and a pitcher going into his windup. Shoot a lineman in a three-point stance (head up, remember), a running back sidestepping a tackler or getting ready to throw a pass, a place kicker poised behind the ball, a punter getting ready to take his first step; don't catch them in the actual process of passing, kicking, or tackling. The same goes for soccer. Have the player holding the ball or getting ready to kick it, not actually throwing or kicking the ball. They may fuss, but they'll be much happier with the final results.

You can get some good ideas on posing athletes by looking

through the game programs or yearbooks of major college or professional teams. These photographs are usually made by well-known professional photographers who travel the circuit every year just for that purpose. If you ever get the chance to watch one of them in action, it's a lot of fun, and you'll get a quick education in photographing athletes.

Don't Forget the Cheerleaders

Many children's teams also have cheerleaders. Don't forget to include them and offer the same package you offer the players—both individual and group photos.

There's a parent who acts as a cheerleader sponsor for each team, and perhaps there is an overall cheerleader coordinator for the entire league. Get them to help pose the youngsters.

American Legion Baseball

While setting up your sports jobs, don't forget about American Legion baseball. While it's definitely not Little League, it still provides some good opportunities. Someone at the American Legion post, or a high school baseball coach, can put you in contact with the right people.

Your town might also have a semipro team, which will also need photos, not necessarily for individuals, but for programs and for publicity purposes.

Good Public Relations

It's always a nice gesture on your part to give a complimentary copy of the team photograph to the coach or the sponsor or both. Children's sports can provide annual jobs for you and can result in other assignments from pleased families as well.

Chapter Ten

Schools, Kindergartens, Preschools, and Day-Care Centers

(The lost art returns)

Back in the good old days before school photographers became so numerous and the competition got so heated, I used to do a lot of work for schools—for their newspapers, annuals, sports, proms, etc. But now the school photographers (the guys representing big, national firms, who come in and do the photos of individual students once a year) are throwing in all sorts of "fringe benefits" in order to get these lucrative student contracts. These "fringe benefits" include giving the school a certain number of "free" black-and-white photographs of school activities for its annual, or a given number of "free" days of photographer's time to do black-and-white photos of anything the school wants.

Some of them are now writing into their school contracts provisions for individual photos and group shots for proms and school dances, as well as athletic teams.

In addition to the school photographers, many high schools now have courses in photography or graphics and their own darkrooms, to which student photographers have access.

For a while such things as these almost killed school business as far as the freelancer was concerned. But there's a bright spot on the horizon! All is not lost.

While most school photographers take a certain amount of care in the way they make the individual student photographs, all the freebies are really a nuisance and a bother for them. Sometimes they'll hire a so-called photographer, usually a kid, to go back to the schools to shoot the "free" pictures.

If the school photographers do such work themselves, getting the film processed and the photos printed and back to the school poses a problem. The national school-picture companies they represent offer, in some cases, to do this black-and-white processing for their people in the field. But all the color processing comes first; thus the black-and-white work is often put off and delayed.

While there are some excellent student photographers in some schools, for every good one there are probably fifteen terrible ones in terms of the results they produce. Many schools are now realizing that having a course in photography or a darkroom students can use doesn't necessarily mean the school will be getting free photographs that are usable. School annual after school annual full of fuzzy-graphs has helped open the door once again for the freelance photographer.

Sports

A lot of coaches, too, are beginning to realize that they might be better off dealing with a local photographer. Most of the time the school photographers are from out of town. Difficulty in getting in touch with them, trouble in coordinating schedules when they may be working fifty to one hundred schools or more, late or extremely slow deliveries, poor quality of work, difficulties in getting remakes set up—these are some of the problems coaches and sponsors of other school activities have been running into frequently in recent years. Many of these school officials now realize they are far better off and have far fewer problems when they deal with reputable local freelance photographers.

Your sports shots for high school athletic teams will be like the ones we discussed in Chapter 9, on children's sports, except your sub-jects will be older, better coordinated, and usually easier to pose. Your equipment, lighting, and poses will be the same. Coaches will usually collect your money from the individual players if you ask them to.

Also check with the coaches early in the year to see if they need either black-and-white or color group shots for programs, posters of the schedule, etc. Some larger schools have an athletic director who can coordinate your work with each of the many different athletic teams. If not, then you'll have to check with the coach of each team.

As far as candid or action sports shots, you'll need these only if you're providing coverage for the school annual or a newspaper. If you're not familiar with this kind of photography, it'll require some practice. The prime rule to remember is to try to catch the action at its peak—a tackler leaping through the air, a basketball just as the player releases it, the goalie stretching to block the ball, etc.

Bands

Photographing bands is probably one of the best ways to get started in school work. Most bands have quite an active booster club made up of parents of band members. They help in many ways, such as raising money for uniforms and for trips to parades and band contests.

The kickoff of the opening game of a new season is a natural for the local weekly newspaper as well as for the school yearbook or newspaper. Schools provide a surprising range of photo opportunities; they can mean big business for the local photographer.

You can offer color group photos of the band, as well as individual photos of members, just the same as for the athletic teams. If you can make contact with the band director or someone active in the booster club, chances are you'll have the opportunity to get this assignment.

Another important fact is that band contests are becoming quite numerous, and they generally move from school to school. If you're the official photographer of your local school band, chances are that when the band contest comes to town, you can get that, too. Action photos of the various units as they're performing, or shots of the musicians lined up to come on the field, are good sellers.

Get the name and address of the director of each band; mail him sample prints after the contest, and ask him to take orders.

Proms and Dances

In photographing these, you'll probably be dealing with a dance committee or a teacher-sponsor. This can be to your benefit, but you'll have to tell them what you want.

In the case of a junior-senior or senior prom, as well as some of the other larger dances like Christmas, the dance committee will do quite a bit of decorating for the event. Be sure to remind them to build a place to be used specially as the background for photos. Tell them not to use colors that are too dark or that will clash with some of the outfits. Also, there shouldn't be too much white, or you might get a bloom from it when the strobe goes off. There especially should be no silver or gold or any other highly reflective surface, such as tin foil, which dance committees like to use in decorations. Also caution the committee against setting you up in front of floral wallpaper or any other busy patterns. Usually a nice neutral color or a soft pastel is best. Greenery and red flowers also blend in quite nicely.

Remind them that you'll need to be in a location, away from the dance floor, where you'll have enough light to focus the camera and see what you're doing. But just in case, always take along a small flashlight. You'll probably need it to check your camera settings from time to time. I've been in some situations that were so dark I had to have the first couple hold a lighted match or cigarette lighter so I could focus on it.

With a piece of masking tape, mark the spot on the floor where you want the couple to stand. It helps if you can start directing by telling them to stand on the tape. Also, make sure you don't get them too close to the background, or you might run into some bad shadows.

The best method for collecting your money is to ask the dance committee or sponsor to take it up at school during the week before the dance. That way when you get there, everything will be prepaid. There may be several couples who didn't want photos and will change their minds after they get to the dance. Collecting that small amount of money on the spot will be no problem.

If the school won't collect the money in advance, ask the committee to furnish students who'll sit at a table, collect the money, and write receipts, so all you'll have to concentrate on is the photos. If you can get a family member or associate to go along with you to help with the money, this won't present a problem, and then you won't have to ask for student help.

Again, this is one of those situations where you only take one shot—in this case, per couple. If you watch the viewfinder closely, you'll be able to see the exact expressions you're recording on film from your strobe. You'll be able to tell if someone closes his eyes or talks or laughs or otherwise messes up just as you press the shutter. Then you can shoot another exposure if you have to.

I like to get set up fairly early at a dance. If it's scheduled to run from eight p.m. until midnight, I'm usually set up by eight. I usually have the understanding that I will shoot from then until ten thirty or eleven, and this announcement is made to the students in advance. I also have the band remind students several times during the dance that "photos are now being taken, and the photographer will be leaving at eleven."

I use the same equipment for photographing proms that I do for dance schools: a 2¼ camera with normal lens and a strobe bounced out of an umbrella, high and directly behind the camera.

If you want to go to the extra cost (be sure to add it to your package price), you can have folders made for the prom sets with the name of the school, the date, and the name of the dance imprinted on them.

As usual, it's a good public relations gesture to provide a free photograph for the sponsor and spouse or for the committee director and date.

Graduation Photos

Photos of seniors in their caps and gowns and a group photo of the graduating class are also good possibilities. You'll need to work this out through the teacher who's the senior class adviser.

It's usually best to arrange to do these before the actual night, or afternoon, of graduation. That's a mighty hectic time. Seniors usually come into school a couple of days the week before graduation to practice for it. Try to make the photos during that time.

These are usually full-length shots, so you'll need a background. In many cases you can use the stage curtains, or you can set up your portable roll-paper background as we discussed in Chapter 8. It adds a nice touch to have the graduate holding a diploma. You can borrow one diploma from the school and use it for every student.

The front steps of the school, if they are large enough, or the bleachers on the football field are usually the best places for the group class photo.

School District Newsletters

I once had a working arrangement with several different school districts, which put out a quarterly newsletter to be sent to the home of each student. My assignment was to travel to each school and photograph the student activities that were featured in the newsletter. This type of job also provides you with an excellent opportunity to make contacts at the various schools for other photo assignments.

Kindergartens, Preschools, and Day-Care Centers

Quite often church and private kindergartens, preschools, and day-care centers are too small for the well-known school photographers. Such organizations offer a good chance for you to move in and pick up a good-paying account.

I've done individual student packages and group photographs for some of these organizations and always found a high percentage of sales in such a market. Here again, I always get my money in advance. I'm not working on a large enough scale to show proofs to the students and then have them order, the way school photographers do.

You'll probably have to pay a commission to the organization for each package you sell, as school photographers do.

In addition to the packages you sell (and in these organizations the percentage of sales is usually high), you can always expect to pick up some more income from reorders. Since these orders are paid for in advance, they represent guaranteed money in the bank.

Pricing and Equipment. There are school-picture labs that will work with freelancers who photograph kindergartens on 120 film, or you can offer the standard prom set: two 5x7s and four wallet-size. If you're photographing class groups, you'll probably want to do this on 120 film also and offer 8x10 prints. While 5x7s are usually best for dance schools, where the classes are small, classes in kindergartens and such will usually contain anywhere from twenty to thirty-five children. The larger print will naturally give you a bigger picture of each child's face.

With so many children in the group, you'll want to shoot several exposures to get a good one. I doubt if you'll ever get a shot without someone making a face and with all of the eyes open, but it's good to have a choice. Make certain that your lab will edit these multiple group exposures to pick the best one.

For the individual photos, you can use the same equipment that you use for all indoor prom sets: 2¼ camera on a tripod and strobe bounced out of an umbrella (you can use one, high and behind the camera, or use a two-umbrella system to give you a side light as well as your main light). You'll need a stool without a back (a sturdy wooden box will do) so that those "little people" will be a convenient height to shoot. In the way of a background, you can use roll paper or one of the smaller canvas or environmental backgrounds that are readily available. Or you can use a regular old-fashioned window shade (see Chapter 25, passport and application photography).

Shooting Early in the Day Is an Advantage. Try to arrange the schedule so you can begin shooting as soon as the school day begins. The children are brighter and more excited then than later in the day, and their clothes are cleaner! It's awfully hard to get a decent photo that parents will appreciate if the youngster is covered from head to toe with finger paint or food stains. Get the teacher to help you check to make certain that all bows are tied, buttons are buttoned, faces clean, and hair in place.

Shooting Early in the Year Is an Advantage. Most individual student photos are best taken in early fall, shortly after the new school year starts. One good thing about such a schedule is that the photos can be delivered before Christmas, when many parents like to give them as gifts or enclose small prints in Christmas cards and letters. This could be a good selling point for you in getting kindergarten, preschool, and day-care center accounts. A school photographer, with many schools, can't possibly do all of the shooting so that every organization will get its prints back before Christmas. It's only natural that they try to get to the big schools first, often putting the smaller ones off until after Christmas, or even as late as early spring.

Make sure that you point out to the director or principal that you can do the work early and guarantee delivery before the Christmas holidays (after first checking with your lab to be sure you aren't making a promise you can't keep).

A reputation for broken promises and late deliveries is one that's very hard to overcome. This is, perhaps, the primary reason for a school photographer losing an account: not being able to deliver what or when he promised.

Little Ones Graduate, Too. Most of these preschools and kindergartens also have graduations, just like the "big people," complete with caps and gowns and diplomas. Here's another chance for individual packages and a class graduation photo. Offer the standard two 5x7s and four wallets, and I guarantee you'll also get a bunch of reprint orders.

Back to School

So, once again, going back to schools can be a worthwhile venture for the local freelance photographer.

Check with the teacher in charge of the school's annual, the principal, the adviser for the school newspaper, the coaching staff of each sport, the band director, and the cheerleading director. Point out to them that you can give fast, reliable, high-quality service—and that you're only a phone call away.

Other possibilities you might want to check out with the school principal are the various honors awarded during the year. They may include a teacher of the year award, honors for outstanding students, sports and band letters, and tokens of recognition for other kinds of accomplishments.

On your black-and-white work, you may have to scale down your prices a little, but it could well be worth it if you get regular business from one or two high schools. On color work—individual packages and group photos for the various activities—school photographers usually charge as much or more than the going freelance price. You won't have to worry about any price reductions here.

Get your foot in the door! Don't let the school photographers and their freebies scare you off any longer. The work is there to be had for the photographer who's nearby and reliable and who can turn out high-quality work.

Chapter Eleven

Commercial and Industrial Photography

(Cover your business community like a blanket)

Once you begin to get your freelance photography business established, you'll probably find that most of your big-money jobs come from commercial and industrial clients. Many beginners overlook the larger business and manufacturing firms as potential clients, assuming that surely businesses this large must produce their own photographs. While it's true that larger companies often have in-house staffs to handle the photographic needs of promotion, publicity, and advertising. I've known many instances where the "staff" consisted of one overworked photographer who couldn't possibly handle all the work that came his way.

It isn't unusual for even some moderate-sized commercial and industrial firms to have annual photographic budgets in the range of $25,000 to $50,000. They may have double that much in their advertising budgets.

Some of these firms will keep an open account with you. You keep track of your charges and bill them monthly. Others will work on an individual purchase-order arrangement. In either event, one customer like this will provide you with enough basic income to take care of all your overhead and give you a good profit as well. Any other business you gain will be gravy.

A friend of mine who's a full-time freelance photographer makes a good part of his annual income by doing work for two nationally and internationally known manufacturing firms who have plants here in Columbia, South Carolina. Both of these plants have in-house photographic staffs, but they call him in to handle their overflow work, and also to handle jobs that are too technically complicated for the staff. Both of these firms also have national advertising agencies that handle all their promotion and advertising, but these firms are in New York and the large pieces of machinery that need to be photographed are in South Carolina. Once the firms determined that there was a local photographer capable of producing the quality of work they demanded, they stopped flying New York photographers in to do the shooting and turned the work over to a hometown photographer.

The moral of this story: Just because a business is large is no reason in itself for you to cross it off your list of potential clients. One reason a business succeeds and grows to a national or international scale is the ability to determine where it can get the goods or services it needs, at the best price for the best quality, in the shortest period of time. Big businesses know what they want and will quickly recognize your ability to produce it. If you can fill the bill, it makes no difference whether your address is New York City, Los Angeles, or Podunk.

While larger firms know what they want, smaller businesses often don't. Some have even overlooked photography entirely; they've never even given a thought to how professional photographs could improve their sales and boost their growth. Here's where your salesmanship can have a chance to shine.

By examining their needs, you can make suggestions and offer services that are uniquely tailored to their individual businesses, and create a good source of revenue for yourself. While many specific types of businesses are discussed in detail in various chapters of this book, here are some general suggestions that apply to many different types of firms and offer unlimited opportunities for job assignments.

Product Shots

All manufacturing firms need photographs ("product shots") of the items they produce. These photos are used in catalogs, catalog updates, and brochures that are mailed out to customers, in presentations by their salespeople, and for advertising in trade publications or newspapers and magazines.

I've done product shots ranging from jewelry to sewing patterns, from screen doors and windows to boats, furniture, and even individual nuts and bolts.

Some of these shots can be tricky and call for a lot of experience or ingenuity. For instance, how do you make a metal screen door seem to stand up by itself in a photograph? I held it up with piano wire, painted black, against a black roll-paper background.

You can do some product shots, mostly small items that can be easily moved, at your own place. It's usually easier if possible to have the items brought to you, because you'll have better control over your background and lighting in your own home. There you can take your time setting up the shots, without being in an unfamiliar environment where other people are going about their jobs at full tilt while you're trying to concentrate on making a photograph.

It's not beautiful or glamorous, but to a firm that manufactures such machinery, it's a mighty important shot. Commercial and industrial photography assignments are available in your own community. Search them out.

A roll-paper background and your strobes bounced out of umbrellas will handle most of these shots. For smaller items, use a card table to bring the subject up to an easy working height. Set up your roll-paper background in the usual way behind the table. Cover the table with a separate piece of paper, cut off from the roll.

There will be times, however, when your product shots will have to be made on location. It's a little difficult to have an eighty-ton rock crusher or a piece of highway construction machinery sent around to your house.

Often you'll be working under some trying conditions at locations that are less than desirable, such as in a warehouse or at the end of the assembly line in the plant. Cluttered, dirty, and unsightly backgrounds can present problems.

There's one easy solution to the problem of backgrounds of this type: Drop out the background entirely. An airbrush artist can easily paint out the entire background, leaving only the subject of the photograph. This same effect can also be achieved by the printer through the use of a mask that leaves only the subject showing in the photo.

As I stated, all manufacturing firms use product shots, but some use them in greater quantities than others. If there's a toy-manufacturing plant in your area, then you'll have a potential mint if you can land that account. It doesn't have to be a big plant, either. There must be literally thousands of stuffed-toy manufacturers located all across the United States. Each one probably produces a hundred or more different animals, and each animal must be photographed in color.

I know of several individuals and small businesses in my area who produce handmade toys, some designed especially for extra-hard use in nursery schools and day-care centers. These people don't do enough volume to have salespeople on the road, so all their selling must be done through the use of photographs.

How to Find Clients

There are many more operations in this category of one-person, family, or mini businesses that need photographs to market their wares. How do you find out about them? Read your local newspapers, especially weeklies. These folks are always good for a feature story from time to time, and newspapers like to print items on local people who are enjoying success.

Another way is to study the Yellow Pages. Every year when the new directory comes out, I sit down and read the Yellow Pages with the same enthusiasm as I would a new bestseller on photography. The Yellow Pages really can provide you with a "bestseller list" of potential clients for your freelance business, giving you many additional leads to follow up on.

Your chamber of commerce will probably have a directory of all the manufacturing firms located in your area. In addition to the names and addresses, and lists of key executives, the directory will tell you what they manufacture. Some chambers also have lists of *all* businesses and industries in their areas, with the same type of information. You'll have to pay for these directories, but they're usually inexpensive and well worth the cost.

If you live in a small town that doesn't have a chamber of commerce, try your county development board or your state industrial development board. They may be listed under slightly different names, but they all do the same type of work and publish the same type of information.

Flyers and Mailers

How about creating an inexpensive flyer that advertises your services as a freelance photographer? Then hand-deliver it or mail it to small businesses in your neighborhood. Make it a prototype for the flyers you'll produce for the local merchants. Try using the same amount of copy and the same number of photographs, and keep the price very reasonable. Local merchants often need these for special promotions and sales.

Sprinkle these around the same way you do your business cards. And, please, use only good-quality photographs, and lots of them. Have you ever noticed how many photographers don't use photographs in their newspaper, magazine, or Yellow Pages advertising? If you're trying to convince people to use photographs in their businesses, for goodness' sake give them a good example to follow!

Brochures

How many brochures are you exposed to in the space of one week? How many do you get in the mail? Have you ever been in a hotel or motel that didn't have a brochure rack prominently displayed or stacks of brochures on the counter? Visit the chamber of commerce office, and you'll probably find a brochure describing every tourist attraction, every festival, and every city or town in your state and the neighboring states. And every one of these brochures is filled with photographs.

Someone had to provide those photos. Why can't you produce a good percentage of them? Because you haven't gone after the brochure business—that's the only reason. You're certainly capable of producing photos just as good as the ones that you'll find in brochures, probably better. It's amazing to sit down with a stack of brochures and see some of the terrible photos that someone paid good money for.

Every hotel, motel, restaurant, church, amusement park, local festival, entertainment facility, golf course, private school, tourist attraction, museum, art gallery, blacksmith, winery, egg farm—you name it—is a potential brochure customer.

All businesses that have stockholders produce annual reports, which are nothing more than fancy brochures. Your city government probably produces one, with photographs. Mine does.

Here's another good point for the freelance photographer: Most photographs used in brochures or annual reports have multiple potential uses for the client, which can result in the sale of many extra prints of each photo. Why sell only one print when you can sell six? Point this out to your client. It's cheaper for him to order all the prints he's going to need at the same time.

Governmental Agencies

Sometimes your local police and fire departments can be sources of new business, especially if you're located in a small to medium-sized city or town. Larger departments have their own photographers, but the smaller ones often need photos of fire or crime scenes, which they call local photographers in to handle.

Some departments also produce their own training manuals and materials, such as slide/sound presentations. It never hurts to ask.

City hall can also be a source. How many proclamations does your mayor sign every year? Is the staff photographer always available to photograph these? Does he always get photos of local officials when visiting dignitaries arrive? Then, too, the staff photographer gets sick and takes vacations just like everyone else. Wouldn't you like to fill in for him? And at your regular fee, of course.

The coroner, the county sheriff, county and city councils, the county and city treasurers—all of these folks need photographs in carrying out their day-to-day operations. Governmental agencies provide a good opportunity for you to get back some of that tax money you've been paying all these years.

Decorative Photography

Have you ever noticed all those murals or large prints that are used to decorate practically every public building, bank, business firm, manufacturing plant, hospital, restaurant, hotel, motel, and private home? Here we go with another of those never-ending lists!

Photography has really come into its own as a first-class method of interior decoration. Photographs used for decoration include everything from beautiful, peaceful landscapes to shots of workers performing the various jobs found in a particular manufacturing plant.

Many firms that cater to tourists (such as hotels, motels, and restaurants) like to decorate with photographs of local scenes of interest to visitors. We have some beautiful gardens in South Carolina, and you'll find photographs of these on display in businesses in many different cities across the entire state. Scenes shot at our beaches are used by businesses from the seacoast to the mountains.

I really can't think of any kind of business firm that couldn't easily use decorative photographs to spruce up its offices, plants, or stores. It's just a matter of selling. Point out to them that, rather than spending their money on art reproductions or original art by lesser artists, they could spend the same amount with you and end up with meaningful photographs that directly relate to their business or the area in which they're located.

Have you considered the possibility of selling local department stores on using large photographic murals in their store displays, or as backgrounds in their street-front windows? Perhaps a beach scene for a bathing suit display, or action at the local football stadium as the background for fall sports clothes, would be appealing to them. The field covered by the term *decorative photography* is really a wide-ranging one, and can provide you with a large list of potential clients.

You might also want to include the general public as possible customers for your arty offerings. I've been in many a place, such as restaurants and gift shops, especially in resort or vacation areas, where local photographers had their work displayed for sale. These prints are usually very attractively mounted and matted and wrapped in plastic for protection. Some art galleries now have photographic sections, and I've even seen local photographs for sale in department stores. If you want to go this route, you'll probably want to take advantage of having your work in local sidewalk art sales and in arts and crafts shows.

Display Photographs

Businesses often need photos for displays at trade shows. If you've ever visited such a show, no doubt you've been impressed by the tremendous numbers of large photographs. Some of the most attractive displays I've seen included large color transparencies. Such specialized photography can produce high profits, especially if you're also retained to help design the display.

If you've ever been to the county or state fair, I'll bet you've seen displays by local firms that included photography. You could have done that—that is, if you'd asked!

Airports are another place where you'll find photographs of local business and industry on display, as are bus stations and train stations. Remember the chapter called Advertising—Display Your Work (Chapter 5)? The same theme holds true for the rest of the business community.

Employee of the Month

Selecting an "employee of the month" (or at some firms an "employee of the week") is a good morale booster for the work force, as many companies have discovered. The honored employee may receive such publicity as having a photograph published in the company newsletter, having a photograph displayed in a prominent place in the office, and being presented with a plaque or certificate, with the ceremony being photographed. In short, the entire proceeding is centered around photographs.

Such an assignment is one of those regular sources of income that can mean much to your freelance business, something you can count on every week or month. Even large firms with in-house staffs don't always have the facilities or equipment necessary for professional portraits.

I received a telephone call one day from a department of our local telephone company. Know what they wanted? They wanted me to provide them with an 8x10 color portrait twelve times a year of their employee of the month—one print for the office and another print for the employee! It wasn't unusual for the employee, after looking at the proofs, to order some additional wallet-size prints or perhaps an extra two or three 5x7s.

In addition, over the years, I've also booked several weddings and family-portrait assignments from these employees.

I'd never have thought to call Southern Bell to ask them to let me photograph their employee of the month, but I'm sure glad they called me. You can bet I got on the phone and began to call a few other firms that I thought might have the same program for their employees. I found some, too! You can find them for your business if you'll make the effort.

Other Business Needs

Even if a business is the rare one that really has no need for advertising or promotional photographs, they certainly have other photo needs in their daily operations. Many businesses are keeping photographic inventories of their equipment these days, for the same reasons that private homeowners are doing it: future insurance claims (see Chapter 15, insurance).

Some plants, big and small, need employee identification cards or security clearance badges. Others maintain an up-to-date photograph in the employee's personnel folder. Still others use photographs in preventive maintenance programs or in maintaining equipment records.

Many firms have their own publications, which use photos for illustrations. These could include training or procedure manuals, instruction manuals for consumers, safety manuals, and so on.

I've done a considerable amount of work for the local plant of an international textile manufacturer. My primary assignment was to photograph new pieces of equipment as they were being installed in the plant. The entire process in use at this plant was top secret in the industry, and each time I entered the plant I had to be checked through security and have a member of plant management with me at all times. The number of rolls of film I had with me was inventoried when I entered and when I left. I was told one day by my escort that this company preferred to use local photographers with known reputations as a precaution to assure that no company secrets were passed on to their competitors. I found this to be amusing at times. I was hired because I had a reputation locally, but my reputation never helped me out a bit when it came to going through those time-consuming security checks on every visit to the plant.

Never overlook your local business community. Even if all the firms are small ones, they can add up to big business for you.

Chapter Twelve

Aerial Photography

(Pick your pilot very carefully)

Do you like to fly in small airplanes? The only difference between taking aerial photos and taking photos on the ground is that you have to be in an airplane for the former. There's certainly no difference in technique or procedure.

But sometimes when you're in the air, you may not be entirely *in* the airplane. You may be hanging part of yourself out the window to get your shot. Fear of flying would, therefore, preclude your making a bushel of money on aerial photographs. If that's your problem, skip this one and proceed directly to the next chapter.

Who Needs Aerial Photos?

You'll have to sell some clients on them; others know before they call you what a tremendous help aerials can be in certain situations. Let me give you a couple of examples of some of my best aerial jobs.

Some years back, Mobil Oil Corporation decided to move into South Carolina, where they hadn't been operating before. They sent in one of their real estate specialists to start looking for sites. He called on a local real estate agent for whom I had done a couple of small aerial jobs, and that's how I made the contact.

Over a period of a couple of years, I took aerial photos of every site in my hometown, and in the central part of the state, that the company was considering for a service station location. They used these photos for many purposes, such as determining how many homes were within a given radius of the site, what traffic arteries were in the vicinity, what grading would be done on the site, and so on. A set of photos of each site consisted of shots from the four compass points, plus a vertical. The company specified the altitude they wanted. This was a goodie! My thanks to Mobil Oil.

One day I called on the superintendent of our school district to ask if he needed an aerial photo of a new school that had just been completed. This one call resulted not only in the assignment for which I'd asked, but an assignment to make aerial photographs of the other nine schools in the district as well.

The contractors who had constructed the schools then wanted copies of these photographs. One contractor wanted his school shot from a different angle than the one I'd used for the school district. He arranged to meet me at the school, landed his private helicopter on the grounds, and took me up to get precisely the angle he wanted.

I took my aerials from a helicopter that day, despite my preference for small airplanes. For one thing, it was a free ride. The price I had quoted (and he agreed on) had also included airplane rental, but I felt that I earned my fee because that little copter scared me to death. Since there weren't any doors, I kept praying that the assembly line worker on this particular machine hadn't failed the course in seat belt installation. Evidently he passed, but I tied the extra piece of seat belt that extended beyond the buckle to my own belt just to be on the safe side.

Industries, shopping centers, shopping center developers, real estate agencies, architects, banks, marinas, oil companies, farmers, ranchers, building contractors, telephone companies, road and bridge contractors, and even private homeowners are included among my aerial photography clients. I'm sure you can think of even more people to call on for this work.

Shoot on Speculation

While you're up in the plane on assignment—going to the site, in the vicinity, or on the way back—shoot a couple of things on speculation. Make up proofs and take them to the firms who own the buildings or land that you've shot. I've sold a lot of aerials in this manner, even though the photographs hadn't been ordered. If they didn't sell, I usually gave the owner the proofs anyway (depending on his response to my sales pitch and his attitude). More often than not I'd get a call at a later date for an aerial or an on-the-ground assignment.

If I had two aerials to do on one flight, I'd usually split the cost of the airplane and pilot rental up among the clients. Many times when I was going up for a single job, I'd call some of my regular aerial customers and tell them I was flying. If they had anything that needed to be done, it would be cheaper then since I was already going to be up. People, including business people, love a bargain. Sometimes they would give me a job to shoot that they wouldn't normally have bothered with, just because it would be a little cheaper than usual.

Advantages and Fees

Don't be afraid of aerials! I'm not referring to the fear of flying. That's something you'll have to overcome by yourself. But there are some photographers who've never taken an aerial photo because they don't know whether or not they have the ability. If you can take a good photograph on the ground, you can take a good photograph from the air. There's really no difference.

Plus, you can charge more for aerials. It's an accepted fact among users of commercial photography; aerials cost more money. And I'm not just talking about the extra cost of plane and pilot. I'm talking about more money per photograph, or a higher hourly rate, whichever way you base your charges. I don't know why this practice ever became established. Maybe the early aerial photographers figured they would charge extra because they were risking life and limb by flying. Regardless of its origin, it's a nice practice, and I wouldn't try to change it.

The Ideal Small Airplane

Notice that I've been talking about *small airplanes.* Most inexperienced aerial photographers tend to think in terms of using a helicopter. *Don't.* They're much more expensive to rent, usually about two to three times more per hour than small airplanes, and they don't make as good airborne platforms for your camera.

"But they hover," you say. "They stand completely still."

Yes and no. They hover, but they don't stand completely still. They vibrate like crazy while they're hovering, and they're extremely hard for the pilot to control when they're hovering. Helicopters aren't as easy as a light plane to slip into a turn for a photograph. And they get cold in the winter when you have to take the doors off to take photos.

For my money, a Cessna 152 is the ideal airplane for aerial photography. This little two-seater—what I like to call the "VW bug of the aircraft industry"—can be throttled back into the thirty- to forty-knot range, and when you're at one thousand feet, for all practical purposes that's almost like standing still. The pilot can *slip* the Cessna into a picture-taking position rather than bank into it. I don't know the technical aspects of piloting a small airplane, but I do know that, whatever's responsible for the Cessna's maneuverability, it's much easier to take aerial shots.

There are two important features that any airplane you choose must have. It must have a window on your side that will open, preferably by swinging out and up toward the wing. By opening that way, the window will be completely out of your way, and the air flow will hold it up so you don't have to keep one hand on the window and the other on

I took these two shots for a client who wanted to show a new building's proximity to the interstate. Many businesses in your town could use aerial photographs. If you can take pictures on the ground, you can take them from the air—and charge more for them!

the camera. That gets a little difficult. The second feature the airplane must have is a high wing—above your field of view, not below it. Your client is paying for a picture of something other than the wing of an airplane.

Don't try to shoot through a window. Some people do, but I've never found a window on an airplane that was clear enough, even if it had just been washed. You're always taking a chance when you shoot through glass. And the way I look at it, just being up in the air is chance enough for me. Why risk fouling up the shot?

Larger planes like the Cessna 172 are nice when you have a job that's some distance away from the airport, or if you need to take the client or a friend with you. This four-seater costs more per hour to rent, but it's considerably faster than the 152. Therefore, your costs will usually be less even though you're paying a higher hourly rate.

A Word of Warning

Before I forget, if you're hired to take photographs of tracts of timberland or a piece of property on a large lake, rent a larger airplane and take the client with you! When you get five hundred or a thousand feet in the air, it's hard to tell one tree from another. When you get over a lake, every cove looks about the same, and all the property has two things in common: It has trees on it, and it fronts on the water! Take it from an experienced photographer who has shot the wrong cove or tract of timberland and has had to rent the airplane and go up again. Let the client pick out what he wants you to shoot. If he makes a mistake, he'll have to pay for it!

"You won't have any trouble identifying this particular piece of land," one real estate client told me. "It has a kidney-shaped fish pond right in the middle of it, surrounded by tall pine trees." Would you believe that in that particular vicinity, there were visible from the air four kidney-shaped fish ponds, all surrounded by tall pine trees! Things aren't so easy to spot when you're not on the ground.

What Camera for Aerial Photography?

Any camera that has a shutter speed of at least 1/500 of a second will do for aerial photography. At one thousand feet or higher, you can get by with 1/250 as far as ground speed goes, but I like to have that little extra insurance of 1/500 in case we hit an air pocket or get a little extra vibration at the time I press the shutter button.

I use 35mm for color slides only. I like to use my Mamiya Press camera for two reasons: First, I like the 2¼x2¾ format, and second, it's easy to hold out the window because it has a handle with a built-in shutter release. Try not to stick your camera out too far. If it gets caught in the airstream, it will be shaken up quite a bit. Also, try not to have your arms touching the window frame or any other part of the airplane while you're shooting. You're more likely to pick up vibrations if your arm is resting on the airplane.

Lenses and Filters

Lenses? Use the normal one for your camera. Telephoto is okay if you have to be a long way from the subject because of restricted air space, because there's a radio tower in the way, or something like that. But remember, any little wiggle is picked up more with a telephoto lens, and they're much harder to hold still. If you wiggle a quarter of an inch at one thousand feet, you may blur your subject or miss it altogether.

Focus? Put it on infinity, and forget about it. If you have to focus at fifteen feet for an aerial photograph, you're in a bunch of trouble!

Filters? A haze filter may help some if it's a little hazy, but not if it's very hazy. If you're already up and it's hazy, try to talk the pilot into staying as low as he can. If you're still on the ground, wait until another day. In the summer, the day after a rain is usually a good time to shoot because rain clears out the haze. In the winter, the day after a cold front passes is usually a nice, haze-free day, if it's not too bumpy a ride. If you *have* to shoot with haze, never shoot into the sun. That just makes it worse.

Postscript

Always keep your seat belt fastened in a small airplane, especially when you're hanging out the window. I'm not trying to be funny; a quick bounce from an air pocket or down-draft is much more severe in a light plane than in an airliner. While it would take a really nasty jolt to toss you out of an open window, it's not hard to bump your head or smash your camera.

Be sure to have a strap on the camera and keep it around your neck. It's not hard to lose your grip on a camera if the plane really starts bouncing around, and a thousand-foot drop is too much of a torture test for any camera to pass.

Chapter Thirteen

Real Estate and Architectural Photography

(Building good business)

Real estate agents, architects, and residential and commercial contractors can be among your best clients. They can all benefit from your services; it's up to you to make the contacts and convince them.

Helping Sell Real Estate

Real estate agents probably depend on photographs as much as or more than any other business. Some residential agents use photos almost exclusively for the initial screening of their listings by potential home buyers. Newspaper advertising is a vital part of their business, and most realtors have found that photos are much more effective in such ads than paragraph after paragraph of type describing the homes.

Have you ever counted the number of real estate agents in your city or town? They usually take up several pages of listings in the Yellow Pages, and each listing can mean more income for you.

If you get to do all of a real estate agency's advertising photography, that account alone could be a big step toward your $25,000 income.

This is one area where you might be able to scale your prices down a little if you get volume work from an agent. On several occasions, I've had them give me their entire listing of homes to photograph. I had photos to take in all sections of town, with no rush deadline, so I could photograph the homes whenever I happened to be in the particular area. Thus I was able to make some good money even though I didn't charge as much per shot as I would have on a smaller job.

I've also worked with real estate agencies that make it a practice to prepare special brochures or booklets of their listings when a new plant or industry announces that it's moving into the area. These printed pieces are mailed to the incoming firm with the request that a booklet be given to each employee who'll be moving in with the new plant.

If you're working with a printer (see Chapter 20 on working with a print shop), you can offer a package deal on such brochures and booklets. If agencies with whom you are working don't do this, suggest it to them.

Getting Started. Many real estate firms have bought Polaroids, cheap 35mm cameras, or even 110 cameras and given them to their agents, who're supposed to be photographers as well as real estate salespeople. You can imagine the kind of results most of them get.

Pick out a couple of good-looking homes. It doesn't make any difference whether they're for sale or not. Make yourself some sharp black-and-white and color prints. Then take them and call on some of the bigger real estate agencies. The difference in quality between the prints you show them and the ones their agents have shot will be obvious to them.

You can use your 35mm camera, if you want, on this type of shot, and usually the normal lens is sufficient for exterior work. If the real estate people want large display prints for their offices, I usually go to a 2¼ camera.

If you offer a price an agency can live with, chances are you'll have yourself another client.

Commercial Real Estate. This is where there's money to be made for the freelance photographer. If you can produce photographs that may help sell an entire shopping center, hotel or motel, industrial plant, apartment complex, or large tract of land, your charges will be more than justified in relation to the commission on such a sale.

Aerial photos of the properties are almost always needed in such transactions. Because of their importance, I've devoted a chapter to aerial photos (see Chapter 12).

Dealing with the Wheeler-Dealers. Most real estate salespeople are wheeler-dealers, especially the successful ones. Many times when they start to really have success in the field, they'll leave to open their own real estate business. Every time this happens to a firm you're working with, you have a new client.

Agencies use a lot of portraits of their salespeople in newspaper advertising. With the turnover rate they have, this can almost be a full-time job if you sign up several firms. Also, each new salesperson needs photos for a real estate license in most states.

Working with Architects

Although photographing a building may look easy, architectural photography is almost a profession unto itself. Your average one- or

Showing the entire building may not be the way to maximum visual impact. The arrangement of the branches in this picture helps draw the eye to the dome and the flags.

two-story building doesn't present much of a problem. But when you get into multistory office buildings and high-rise apartment buildings, then you need much more technical expertise. For such work you'll need a view camera that tilts and swings for correcting vertical and horizontal lines. Better get yourself a book specializing in architectural photography and study up.

Back to your average, run-of-the-mill building. In addition to overall views of the structure to show it off to the best advantage, always include a couple of semi-close-ups of some of the more distinctive features, such as an enclosed courtyard, an unusual entrance, distinctive window treatments, etc. Try to find an angle that will eliminate power lines and power poles if possible. By shooting on the weekends, especially on Sunday, you can also eliminate cars which may be parked in front of the building, if this is important to the client.

You'll find architects listed in the Yellow Pages.

Contractors

They range from residential remodeling contractors up through those who build apartment complexes, industrial plants, and high-rise buildings. Many contractors use photographs to keep track of their advances on jobs in progress, especially when they're working for out-of-town clients. They may hire you to make one or two photographs every week for the duration of the job, either from the ground or aerially.

A weekly newspaper wanted a little different construction photo.

Many of them also maintain portfolios of completed jobs. Show them your samples and ask for assignments.

Interior Decorators

This can be another lucrative field because decorators use photographs a great deal. Practically every customer who comes to them brings in one or more photographs cut out of a magazine to show what he thinks he wants. Decorators also like to whip out photographs of their past jobs to show to new and prospective clients. You can also usually sell copies of photos you've done for a decorator to the client for whom the decorator was working.

A 2¼ camera is fine for interior shots. Your wide-angle lens will come in handy since you're working in a confined space and since decorators usually like to get as much of a room in one shot as they possibly can.

Lighting can often be accomplished with available light or a combination of available light and bounced strobe.

Landscape Contractors

These folks also like to maintain photo files of jobs they've done. They may want pictures when they first complete their work, and then additional photographs some months later, when all the plants and grass are really established.

Since you're dealing with wide-open spaces, the 2¼x2¾ camera format is ideal for such shots.

In all exterior photographic situations, you'll find that some shots are definitely morning shots and others are definitely afternoon shots, depending on the direction and angle of the sun. There will be times when you'll arrive on the scene and find that it isn't the correct time of day for that particular photograph. Don't go ahead and try to force the shot. Come back when the sun is right. It may take more time and cost you an extra trip, but the results of doing it correctly will pay off.

Every facet of real estate and building is just crammed full of potential jobs for the freelance photographer. Whether the real estate firms or contractors are large or small, residential or commercial, they all need and use photographs. You can get your share if you'll just put forth the effort to make the proper contacts.

Chapter Fourteen

Shopping Centers, Department Stores, and Models

(They can help you ring up sales)

The phenomenal growth of shopping centers has been a boon for freelance photographers. Every time one springs up, it's like a new little town with job opportunities galore.

A larger shopping center usually has its own merchants' association, a miniature chamber of commerce designed specifically to boost the business of individual merchants in the center by promoting the center as a whole. They're forever staging customer-participation contests of all kinds, and displays such as boat shows, automobile shows, art shows, antique shows, circuses, and arts and crafts fairs.

Sometimes they have a paid executive secretary or director to administer the affairs of the association and the shopping center. If they don't have a paid staffer, the merchant who's been elected president of the organization runs the show. Regardless of who's in charge, that person is a valuable contact for you.

Worth News Coverage?

Shopping centers believe that each event they stage is unquestionably of prime news value. However, weekly and daily newspapers don't always take that same attitude. While daily newspapers often won't even consider occupying any of their space with such activities, a weekly newspaper will run the items—especially if merchants in the center advertise with it, or if the paper is trying to line up more advertisers from the shopping center.

However, weekly newspapers, as stated before, have very limited staffs. Many of them depend to a large extent on having people from outside bring in copy and photographs. They're usually very glad to get what's brought in and will run just about everything.

Therein lies your opportunity! Suggest to the shopping center director that the organization contract with you to shoot photos of all contest winners and of all displays or shows of any consequence. The shopping center can then write a story to go along with your photos, deliver them to the newspaper, and get that free publicity they're all so eager for.

If you know how to write newspaper copy, you can do the whole job and get paid for writing and photography. If you're so inclined, contact shopping centers that don't have paid staffers and offer to handle all their public relations. Merchant presidents usually have their hands full trying to operate their own businesses and need that kind of help.

Be a Part of the Show. When the shopping center has an activity such as an auto or boat show, art or antique show, country fair, or antique car show, also check with each exhibitor on the possibility of taking a color photo of his particular display. You can sell a lot of extra prints this way.

And check with the center to ask about a display of your photos to go along with the show. Photos fit in with anything.

Check with Individual Shop Owners. Make the rounds of the individual shops and stores in the shopping center periodically, and leave your business card with their managers. Some possibilities you can suggest are photographs of any special display the store might have, photos of new employees or winners of any individual contests the store may sponsor, photos of the store's manager to go along with any news releases or announcements, and photographs to use in connection with newspaper advertising, brochures, and the like.

Shopping Center Advertising. Merchants' associations spend a set percentage of the dues they take in from each store to advertise and promote the entire center. Many photos are used in such advertising: black-and-white for newspaper and color slides for television. Don't overlook this possibility.

Department Stores

Large department stores offer many of the same opportunities for work that you'll find in shopping centers.

One important additional factor is that such department stores, some of which are in the heart of the city and not in the shopping centers, usually depend a great deal more on attractive window displays to bring in customers *off the street*. These displays are changed quite often. Many stores like to keep a photographic record of their window displays—another job possibility!

How to Shoot Window Displays. In shooting window displays, glare and reflections in the glass are your two worst enemies. The best method is to shoot windows at night, thus eliminating the glare from the sun and from cars parked near the windows. At night all you have to worry about are car headlights and streetlights. These problems can be solved very simply by purchasing a large piece of heavy, black cloth. Stretch it out behind the camera and between the window and any possible extraneous light sources. You can use your three or four light stands to support the cloth. Put your camera on a tripod, determine the proper time exposure, and you're all set. You might also want to use a polarizing filter as a help in eliminating glare and reflections, especially if you have to shoot in the daylight.

Fashion Shows

Many large department stores stage regular fashion shows for their customers, and many of them like to have a photographer on hand to cover the events.

In fashion shows, models usually pause several times along the runway, pose, and then proceed to the next stop. Make sure you work things out with the person in charge of the show so that the models have a predetermined spot where they'll stop, turn toward the camera, and strike a pose. It's awful hard to try to run along the runway with a model, wait for her to stop somewhere, try to focus, and get a decent shot before she moves on and the next model appears on the scene. By having a predetermined spot, you can prefocus on that spot and wait for the action to come to you.

I prefer my 2¼ camera for this type of photography. You can use a hand-held strobe for lighting, or if the layout is suitable, you can set up your umbrella. You'll have to make sure your strobe battery is fresh. Action on the runway is fast and furious, and you won't have time to wait for a weak battery to recharge.

Fashion Shots for Advertising

Many department stores and boutiques use fashion photography in their advertising, both newspaper and television. A couple of accounts such as these, who'll use you on a regular basis, can provide some pretty good spending money!

At times they use shots taken during fashion shows, but they usually prefer to concentrate on a shot featuring just the right model, in just the right location, with just the right pose to show off the clothes to the best advantage. Such location shots are often made in a park, on the steps of a large office building, on a spiral stairway, or in an old hotel or restaurant. Usually the store will send someone out with you and the model to direct the shooting session and get the desired results for the advertising piece.

Often the store won't come through with budgets for these assignments that are large enough to allow you to hire professional models. All too often the stores will use their clerks, high school students who are on the store's fashion board, or members of the garden club. It would be good for you to take the time to study some of the fashion magazines and the poses they use. You might also want to visit a modeling school (which is another job possibility that I'll discuss later) and get someone there to show you what looks good and to tell you why it looks good. Some time spent in advance study and research will be time well spent if you intend to do fashion photography. Do some practice shots with your wife, daughter, or girl friend. You don't need fancy clothes for these shots; all you're after is proper posing.

Roll-Paper Background. When using background paper, you need to have it suspended from high behind the model and extending almost to the camera (see Chapter 8). This paper can get to be an expensive item, so figure it into your costs when you make up your job quote. It helps to have models tape the bottom of their shoes with masking tape, but don't let the tape show on the sides. This can help keep the paper clean so you can use it for more than one shot. Background paper with dusty footprints doesn't do much for a fashion photograph.

Don't Be Bashful. Some freelance photographers are a bit awed when first beginning to work with professional models. They figure the models know their business, and so they're reluctant to suggest a change in a pose, or to point out that something doesn't look right. They'll just go ahead and shoot.

Don't! Often a model will automatically strike a pose—any pose that comes into her head—and will expect the photographer to change her position or her mood. If you don't like what you see, change it! After all, you're the one who'll be held responsible for the finished print, not the model.

If you're ordered by someone from the store to shoot something that doesn't look right to you, do it. Then do it the way you think would be best, and give them both prints for a final decision. Nine times out of ten yours will be the one the art or advertising director will pick! If it's not, don't worry about it. Just give them the best professional work you can turn out, and the account will be yours for as long as you want it.

Model Agencies and Schools

Every model who works for an agency, or freelances for herself, has to have a portfolio. Some of them can't afford to spend very much

Working with models, you'll often find individual strong features, which may be good or bad for certain shots. This particular model has a long, slender neck. The photos at left emphasize this feature, while the treatments shown on the right play it down.

money, but they realize they have to have professional photographs in order to book good jobs. If you like to photograph pretty girls and women, and make a little money in the process, there's an opportunity waiting for you at modeling schools and agencies.

Many dance schools also offer courses in modeling for those who want to be professionals, or for young women who want to learn such things as stage presence, how to apply makeup, how to dress, how to walk, and just how to look their best. These, as well as other small to medium-sized schools, offer the best chance for the freelance photographer. Many of the larger schools and agencies have their own staff photographers, or have longtime working agreements with studio photographers.

Visit the schools and show them your work. You never know when you'll walk in on a director who's looking for a photographer.

An ad placed in the classified section offering to do portfolios for models will usually bring you some inquiries.

Equipment. Your 2¼ camera will be your mainstay for photographing models. Your strobe and umbrella and a roll-paper background will be the key tools for indoor shooting. You'll also need a few props, such as some large, floppy hats, a large potted plant or two, a dressing table stool, perhaps a wrought-iron chair—mostly things you can find around the house.

Outdoors you'll want to use flash fill most of the time to insure even lighting on the face and arms. Shooting models is really no different from regular portraits, except that most of your shots will be full figure rather than just head and shoulders.

How Do You Learn? There are literally hundreds of good books written on the subject of working with models—some written by photographers and some written by models. You'll find them in your camera store, in ads in photography magazines, in your bookstore, and even perhaps at your local library.

Another good way to learn is to approach the director of a modeling school, maybe the one who also runs the dance school that you're now photographing. Offer to trade some shots for some instruction on photographing the students. Point out to the director that while you're learning, the students will be also. And the school will be getting free photographs for advertising, or for some of the students who find it financially difficult to put together a portfolio.

The Portfolio. As I said, a lot of young models just getting started can't afford to spend a lot of money, but you can offer them cheaper prices than the studio photographer.

Every shot doesn't have to be in color, but a few need to be. Prints are usually 11x14, with some 8x10s sprinkled in. The color shots can be 8x10. Shoot several rolls of black-and-white and one roll of color. Do proof sheets and let the model pick what she wants. Offer her a set number of prints for a set price.

She'll need several changes of clothing. The portfolio should include sports clothes, bathing suit, tennis outfit, evening clothes, a couple of different hats (big, floppy ones usually work well), pants, and other outfits.

You'll need full-figure shots, facial close-ups, action shots, and reclining shots; mix them up.

You'll want to do some shots outside and some inside. Scout around for good locations; parks, public buildings, riverbanks, lakes, and children's playgrounds offer some interesting possibilities. Circular stairways are always good. Try some dramatic locations, such as a building construction site, a piece of heavy highway construction equipment, an old, abandoned building, or the old cannon in the park or in front of the armory. Pretty girls in unusual settings, where you wouldn't normally expect to find them, are always attention getters.

If the model likes the way you work, no doubt she'll recommend you to some of her friends who also want to be models. And when she starts getting bookings, she'll recommend you to some of her clients.

If you can get hired by a school, there'll be some good volume. I've also had modeling schools ask me to come in and lecture on photography, working with models, posing, etc. Some schedule in-school photographic sessions as part of their course.

This is fun work! Models are usually bright and cheery, full of enthusiasm, and, let's face it, very pretty. And you get paid, too!

Chapter Fifteen

Insurance Photography

(This time you collect the premium)

If you're the victim of a fire or burglary, an insurance company will reimburse you only for items you can document. Right now, lay this book down and try to visualize all the valuable items in your bedroom. How about the den, kitchen, living room, even the attic? Do you have the serial numbers of your television, stereo, electrical appliances, and other valuables written down somewhere? How about any collections you might have? Can you list every item in them?

Well? We've just discovered another great way to make money with your camera. How could an insurance company argue with a photographic inventory of everything that's covered by the policy on a home or business? With a photographic inventory, the owner can help the insurance adjuster determine the value of the loss more accurately than with just a list of serial numbers or a written description of the items.

For this reason, many people have gone to a system of photographing their possessions and filing the photos away in a safety deposit box. If a home or business is completely destroyed by fire, storm, or flood, it helps a great deal not to have to worry about which items were (and which were not) reported as lost to the insurance company.

You can create a new source of revenue by offering to come to a person's home or business and photograph his possessions, room by room—even drawer by drawer or item by item if they want. One photographer I know printed up a one-page flyer advertising this service and his fees and left it with some local insurance agents that he knew. The response was good, and he now has another profitable addition to his freelance business.

Two young housewives in my hometown recently started such a photographic business, and this is the only type of work they do. They run their business part-time, and this gives them extra income while allowing plenty of time to be with their families. Working out of their homes, they started the business with a minimal investment (just photo equipment).

Equipment

The 35mm camera is ideal for this type of work. You don't want to be hauling around any more equipment than you actually need. Your normal lens will handle most of the shooting, but a wide-angle lens would come in handy if you want to show most of an entire room in one shot. For photographing very small items, such as coins or stamps, you may want to investigate using a macro lens, or at least a set of close-up attachments for your normal lens.

A single strobe on the camera will take care of most of your lighting needs. On wide shots, and on items that would cause a glare (shiny appliances, TV screens, etc.), you will probably want to bounce the light off the ceiling. When you start photographing individual items, it would be good to have an umbrella and bounce your light out of it. In this case you'll need a light stand to hold the umbrella, and you might also want to take your tripod along.

You'll also want to include the filters we discussed in the chapter on equipment (Chapter 2): a fluorescent-light filter, a tungsten-light filter (depending on the type of lighting), and a polarizing filter.

Film

You'll want to use slide film for this type of photography. Color slides are ideal for a photographic inventory for many reasons. They take up much less space and are easier to handle than large prints. Slides can be easily stored in the limited space of a safety deposit box, while leaving room for other important items. Even though it's small, a 35mm slide can be projected and enlarged many times its size to show the contents of a drawer, or individual coins or stamps in a collection, including dates and mint marks. Slides can be easily and cheaply duplicated in the event the customer wants more than one set to keep in more than one place so he'll always have a copy of the photographic inventory available. Slides are also much cheaper, both for you and the customer, than color prints in a size large enough for items to be easily identified.

Collections and Inventories

In the event that someone has a valuable collection of coins, art, firearms, stamps, silver, or the like, a photographic inventory becomes even more valuable.

Trying to collect on a claim, a fisherman might have trouble explaining to an insurance firm how one rod and reel and one tackle box of lures could be worth hundreds of dollars. But with a photo like this on file, he could document the cost of the box and its contents as well as the rod and reel.

Some artists also use these to keep track of which paintings they've sent to which shows or galleries. I had one artist as a customer who always wanted a slide of each painting before it was framed and one after it was framed. This gave him a visual record of each painting he had sold and the molding he had chosen for it, and also a record in case of fire or theft.

Sportsmen are another good source for such an inventory. If you're not an avid fisherman, it would be hard to convince you—or an insurance adjuster—how much money might be tied up in just one tackle box full of lures. The value could easily reach hundreds of dollars. Dedicated anglers also have a small fortune invested in rods and reels. Can you imagine how much it costs to outfit a family of four to go camping? It's not unusual for a hunter to spend hundreds on a single rifle or shotgun, and a firearms collector may have thousands of dollars tied up in one piece. Sportsmen are very good prospects!

Where Do You Find Customers?

Local insurance agencies, coin and art dealers, sporting goods shops—all of these are good places to look for contacts for such jobs.

When you start inquiring about who has good collections that are also valuable, it's best that the people you ask know who you are first. Start with merchants and insurance people you know personally—and who know your good reputation. Ask them for leads, and leave copies of your flyer or business card.

You might also check with your local police department and sheriff. Tell them you're offering this service. They may provide you with the names of some potential customers and may even help you promote the service in connection with their crime prevention program, the same way they promote use of engravers to identify equipment like TVs, stereos, cameras, and anything else that can be easily stolen and resold.

Don't Forget Apartment Dwellers. Just because a person doesn't own his own home doesn't mean he doesn't need photographic inventories. There's a policy designed especially to cover the items owned by people who live in apartments.

A large apartment complex could provide you with several different customers. Talk with the manager, and ask if you can leave some of your flyers in the office and in the community or party room.

Exterior Photos for Fire Insurance

If you live in a region that's plagued by fire hazards, you may be able to help local home owners and create another source of business for yourself.

In areas of heavy brush and those where the fire hazard is high, home owners pay high premiums for fire insurance. They can get some reduction on these premiums if they're conscientious and clear away all the brush and flammable debris from around their homes. Insurance companies usually need photographic proof of the condition of brush around a home before they can establish premiums. Check with your local insurance agent to see if such areas exist near you. If they do, you may be able to work with an insurance agent, taking photos of home owners' properties, which can be used to get their premiums reduced.

Storm Damage

After any type of serious storm or flood, check around to see if anyone needs photos for insurance claim purposes—airports, marinas, businesses, individual homeowners. This can be a real service to your community as well as a money-making opportunity. That's a good combination.

Accidents

Any time you see an accident, stop and photograph it. This could be an auto-auto, auto-motorcycle, auto-bicycle, auto-pedestrian, auto-train, auto-building, or even a single-auto accident. If the victims aren't injured, tell them you've photographed the scene and that these photos are available to them. Leave your business card. If they're injured, try to get names and addresses and contact them later. The victims may need these photos for either legal or insurance purposes, or both.

Ask Questions

The next time you have occasion to visit your insurance agent to discuss automobile or home owner's insurance, ask if he knows additional ways your photographic services could be helpful in connection with insurance. He might have some suggestions for you.

It wouldn't hurt to visit an agent who deals primarily in business and commercial insurance also. Their clients have very specialized needs in such areas as preventing lawsuits, documentation for worker's compensation and OSHA requirements, and so on. For instance, some companies that insure plate glass windows in stores and businesses require photographs to be submitted with the application for insurance.

Insurance work can be a very profitable part of your business. Like anything else, you've got to take the time and expend the effort to get that business. Once you've established your reputation in a particular area, business will probably come looking for you.

Chapter Sixteen

Family Portraits

(Offer a package deal)

Most families put it off, but eventually they get around to having family portraits taken. And every time there's a new family member added, there's the need for a new family portrait. Especially around holiday seasons, family portraits can be a big part of your business, if you take the time to promote them. They are quite easy to work into your schedule and take little time. The earnings will go a long way toward supporting your own family.

I've found that many families prefer to have their portraits made in their own homes or in their own yards. Seems logical, doesn't it? People always act and look more natural when they're in familiar surroundings. Since they're right at home while you're working, some may even decide to include the family pet—or maybe to have a separate portrait made of the pet, and perhaps one or more separate portraits of each of the children.

You'll want to place an occasional ad in the weekly newspaper promoting your family portraits made "on location." Play up the fact that the entire family won't have to pile in the car and go to a studio; in fact, they won't even have to leave home.

I usually charge an initial fee, which covers the first portrait, travel expenses, and other shooting costs. Then I go to my regular reprint prices if the family needs additional copies of the group shot. If they have additional individual portraits made at the same time, I usually give a price break on these.

Often you'll be able to sell large color portraits, 11x14 being the smallest size I recommend for a wall hanging. The 16x20s and 20x24s are not at all uncommon. Naturally, you'll want to use at least a 2¼ camera, and I often go to the 2¼x2¾ for large family groups.

Outdoor Portraits

I've always liked these. In modern terms, we call them environ-mental portraits. The funny thing is that a lot of drugstore and depart-ment store photographers—and even a lot of the bigger portrait studios—are using elaborate painted canvas or even front-screen projection of outdoor scenes for backgrounds, so *they can make their environmental portraits indoors!* Can you figure that one out?

I'll never forget one of the first outdoor family portraits I made. The family wanted it taken in their backyard, but depended on me to select the location. When I arrived, the first thing I spotted was a split-rail fence along one side of the yard. There was a vacant lot next to it, just full of goldenrod, and it was really gold. There was no question about location. I used that portrait as one of my samples for many years and even printed it in a brochure advertising my services.

Woodpiles are great backgrounds. Stone fences, wrought-iron gates, swings, patios, birdbaths, trees—every yard has something that would make an ideal location for an outdoor family portrait.

Always consider a flash fill to take any small shadows off the faces and add sparkle to the eyes!

Indoor Portraits

My trusty umbrella again provides the lighting indoors, some-times with the addition of another umbrella, especially for large groups. You can buy a little attachment that will allow you to connect two or three sync cords to your camera. These can be used with extension sync cords, which come in lengths of ten feet or longer. Or you can fire the second unit with a slave tripper.

Your biggest challenge is to catch everyone with their eyes open and decent expressions on their faces. I've had some family portraits with as many as eighteen people in them! Film is by far the smallest expense on your list; shoot lots of it. You'll just have to go back and reshoot if someone has his eyes closed or his tongue stuck out in every shot. I always try to concentrate on the youngest children, figuring I can count on the adults to hold a smile longer—but not always. Sometimes the adults are more trouble than the children. It's hard to look at eigh-teen faces at the same time when you're getting ready to shoot. You'll just have to take a lot of shots and hope for the best.

What to Wear. You'll get a lot of questions about what clothes to wear. It really doesn't make a lot of difference, except that they stay away from wild plaids and outlandish colors. I do suggest that all members of the family dress in the same type of clothes for the portrait. For instance, you wouldn't want half of them in formal wear and half in jeans. If they want a formal portrait, they should all be dressed formally. If they want a casual portrait, all should be dressed casually.

For the individual portraits, they can wear anything they like. This is one advantage of shooting portraits in the home; the wardrobe is right there, and they can change clothes as much as they like.

Christmas Cards

Don't forget Christmas cards as an added service and extra income. Even if you shoot a family portrait in March, be sure to suggest they might like to use it on their Christmas cards. You can find many labs that will make up the cards; all you have to do is suggest it to your clients and take the orders. Labs will usually provide you with samples of the different card styles they have available.

Christmas cards are printed from negatives, so if the family wants to order their own, they'll have to have your negative. Make sure you add in an extra charge when you sell that. Remember that the negative rights always belong to the photographer unless specifically requested by the client, who pays an additional charge for them.

Christmas Presents

You should also ask each family if they want to consider extra prints of the portrait to give as Christmas presents. Some of them will probably think of doing this, but they usually won't think of it until a week or two before Christmas, when there's not enough time left to get the prints made.

Labs always get bogged down around Christmas, so keep this in mind when you promise to have the prints ready to use for gifts. Some labs won't guarantee Christmas delivery for portrait orders taken after December 1. I'd rather lose an order than guarantee the customer it'll be ready for Christmas and then not be able to deliver. If you make a promise that you can't keep, you'll likely end up losing the customer for good, which is much worse than losing just that one order.

You should also keep other important dates and holidays in mind to suggest to your customers as occasions for more prints. Family portraits are excellent gifts for Mother's Day, Father's Day, birthdays, and anniversaries.

Candid Portraits of Children

Rule number one is: Never tell a small child to smile! Children don't know how to *make* a smile when ordered to. Smiling is something that just comes naturally to them; it's not a function they can always perform on command. If you tell a small child to smile, what you'll usually get is a screwed-up facial expression—maybe with a tongue sticking out—that doesn't come close to resembling what you want.

The best way to get children to smile is just to talk to them and let them talk to you. Ask them questions like these:

"Show me how big a giant ice cream cone is."

"What do you like to eat when you go to McDonald's?"

"Do you love Santa Claus?"

"Show me how your mommy and daddy look when they're happy."

This kind of easygoing conversation will usually bring the response you want.

In the case of very young children, hanging or holding their favorite toys in front of the camera usually works. Try using hand puppets, or throwing them a ball.

Sometimes Parents Cause Problems. I've had parents tell children such things as:

"If you don't smile, I'm going to blister your bottom."

"That photographer's going to get you if you don't smile."

"Wait till we get home, and I'll take care of you for not smiling."

Needless to say, this is never any help in trying to get decent photos of the youngsters. I don't hesitate to ask a parent to leave the room if I feel this will give me a better working relationship with the child.

Who Says You Always Need a Smile? Some of the best portraits I've ever done of children, including my own, didn't feature even the trace of a smile. Who says you've got to have a grin that runs from ear to ear in order to have a good portrait? Children aren't always happy and laughing. Sometimes they're serious; they're always thinking and learning. Sure, I like happy portraits, but I also like serious studies, especially of young people.

Take your camera and just follow a small child around the yard. Hand him a pebble or a flower to examine. Watch children playing in a sandbox or with dolls and trucks and toy people. You'll see a lot of interesting expressions that don't include a smile.

Another tip: Make your camera as inconspicuous as possible. Don't call attention to it. None of this "watch the birdie" stuff. Just talk to the child about things that will interest him or her. Talk about games he likes to play, favorite toys, pets, friends, and family.

Why Just One Portrait?

Especially in the case of young children, I've often sold the family on the idea of a composite of several smaller prints instead of just one

In the photo above, the child is examining a rock I handed her to take her mind off the camera. Both of these pictures show pretty well that your subjects don't always have to smile or look directly into the camera to make a portrait a family will always cherish.

big one. This way I can offer them several different expressions, several different moods that they recognize, moods they know and love. Big portraits are fine when children get older, but when they're young and so precious, why not try to capture a little more of that by using more than just one shot?

I'll guarantee that parents will love a composite when they see it. Sometimes when I haven't been able to sell the parents on the idea, I'll make a composite of the proofs and take that along when I deliver the bigger print. I've only missed one sale when I went to this extra trouble.

You can either have a lab print a composite of three, four, five, or six poses on the same piece of paper, or buy precut mats that have different numbers of openings for you to insert prints in. I've seen mats with one opening for a 5x7 print and four openings for 4x5 or 3x5 prints. They come with many different combinations of openings.

Presenting Your Proofs

You know how important packaging is! Just think about the items you buy at the supermarket. When there are several different brands of the same product to choose from, how many times have you bought the one that was in the nicest package or had the prettiest label? So many times photographers cram their proofs into a 5x7 envelope, or even into a paper bag, for delivery to the client. Take a little pride in your work! Invest in some proof folders. They don't cost very much, and they give a much more professional appearance to your work. You can use a proof folder more than once; so it may cost you only a few pennies each time. The impression it'll make will be worth a lot more in extra sales than the little extra investment.

The same is true with your finished orders. Always put portraits in a folder. I usually put commercial and industrial shots in folders also.

On most individual portraits of adults, you'll want to have the negatives retouched before the finished prints are made. On women a good foundation or base can do a lot to hide blemishes, but it won't help on lines or bags under the eyes. These can only be removed by the expertise of a skilled retoucher, which most color labs have.

Chapter Seventeen

Garden Clubs

(A profitable arrangement)

Flowers give you the opportunity to put a little "art" into your work. A close-up in living color of an individual bloom or a well-organized arrangement needs very little interpretation or technique to make it a beautiful photograph.

Your Business Will Blossom

Growing flowers and arranging them have come to be important activities in the lives of many people. And they can provide you with still another chance to ply your trade.

Many garden clubs sponsor quarterly, semiannual, or annual flower shows, which attract quite a bit of interest and quite a few participants. Garden club councils, the overall organizations made up of a number of individual clubs, usually sponsor at least one very big show a year.

Contact the president of a garden club or the council. They might like to have a photographer at the next show to photograph the winning entries. Chances are some of the contestants who didn't win would like beautiful color photos of their entries also.

You'll find that a flower show is usually a part of each county or state fair. A phone call to the fair officials might result in your being named official photographer for the fair. If not, you can get the name of each exhibitor by looking at the official entry form displayed at the exhibit. In larger fairs there are both commercial and individual divisions. Call the exhibitors and ask if they would like professional photographs of their exhibits. You could end up with several assignments, all in one location.

Equipment

I usually shoot these assignments with my 2¼ camera, unless I'm going strictly after color slides of the flowers. The normal lens will be fine for arrangements. To capture individual blossoms, a nominal telephoto would be helpful, or a set of close-up attachments for your normal lens.

Lighting

If possible, place the flowers by a window and use the available sunlight. Remember that cross-lighting (or raking light) will bring out the texture of the petals and leaves, giving you a beautiful effect. If you have to use your strobe, bounce the light off the ceiling or a wall. If there isn't a ceiling or a wall handy, have someone hold a piece of white cardboard slightly off to the side of the arrangement and bounce your strobe off this.

Composition

The first rule is: Never reposition any elements of a prize-winning arrangement. Remember, the prize was awarded for the position in which the flowers were placed, and you'll incur the wrath of the arranger if you touch a single stem.

With your composition already taken care of, about the biggest thing you have to concentrate on is the background. You want to place all the emphasis on the flowers themselves; therefore, the plainer the background the better. A soft background of light pastel usually sets off an arrangement to the best advantage. Don't use floral wallpaper, or bricks, or anything busy. Avoid even the suggestion of clutter.

If you're doing a garden shot, include in the foreground an overhanging branch or a few leaves on the tip of the branch. Frame a landscape shot with trees in the foreground. It can sometimes be quite effective to have these trees slightly out of focus. Try to catch an insect or butterfly on an individual flower to add a point of interest.

Clubs Need Programs

The program chairman of each garden club is usually on the lookout for good ideas for future meetings. Offer to provide your local garden club with a program on how to photograph flowers on a strictly amateur basis. Give them good tips on such things as lighting, cameras, lenses, and composition.

Not many of them know how close they can get to an individual flower with the fixed lens on an inexpensive camera. Whether they have

This is the perfect example of how *not* to shoot a flower arrangement. The wrinkles in the background material are more arresting than the flowers. The lighting has thrown the container into complete shadow, making the flowers look as though they were growing out of a black blob. The background should complement the subject, not detract from it.

A plain background insures that the viewer's full attention is on the flower arrangement. Using a top light enhances the texture of the flowers and leaves. The resulting low-key shadow around the base of the arrangement adds an interesting touch to the photo.

expensive and sophisticated cameras or completely automatic cameras, it never hurts to go over the basics with them. Some won't know how to use these cameras either, and if they do, everyone can use a little additional instruction. Show them how to hold the camera to avoid getting motion and blurred pictures. Tell them how close and how far away they can expect to get good pictures with flash cubes. Tell them how to judge if there's enough light outside to get good pictures with their small cameras. You might suggest some of the Kodak publications that contain even more information for the amateur photographer. There are so many hints you could give them that they'd appreciate.

You might also suggest to them the possibility of decorating their homes with professional photographs of their own arrangements out of their own gardens. This way they can enjoy the beauty they have produced for years to come, even during the long winter months when everything outside is bleak and bare. Then show them some of your own outstanding samples of flower photographs, including color slides and color prints. You might get some orders right on the spot.

Some Have Magazines. Many large clubs, councils, or statewide organizations also produce monthly or quarterly magazines, which need photographs both of plants and of people. Most of these will be black-and-white, but some larger magazines also use color.

If you can help garden club members appreciate color photographs of their lovely flowers as much as they appreciate the flowers themselves, chances are that when they have an outstanding bloom or arrangement, you'll get a telephone call and a request for your services.

Chapter Eighteen

Churches and Synagogues

(A good source of business)

I've done a wide variety of photographic work for churches and synagogues in our community, and some of it might surprise you. True, a lot
of congregations have members who're photographers and who'll volunteer their services, but many churches don't.

Confirmation Classes

Each church has a confirmation class of young people who have
reached the age when they're eligible to become regular members. They
go through a series of sessions conducted by the minister, and one Sunday is reserved as Confirmation Sunday, when they're officially admit-
ted to the church.

This usually calls for a group shot of the entire class, and many
families want individual photos of the young people as well. It's best to
take these at the altar after the service. Prom sets, or 8x10s, of the
individuals can be offered. Most prom set orders call for a minimum of
twenty-four negatives to be sent to the lab in order to qualify for that
special price, and many classes are not this large. You can usually get
fewer than twenty-four negatives processed for prom sets, but they'll
cost you more if you're under the minimum.

The group shots are usually 8x10. I prefer the 2¼x2¾ negative for
these large group shots because of the number of people in the photograph. I use a single, hand-held strobe. For the individual shots I use an
umbrella and my 2¼ camera.

Bar Mitzvahs

In the Jewish faith, a bar mitzvah is similar to confirmation.
When a boy turns thirteen, he becomes a member of his religion and the

synagogue in such a ceremony. This ceremony is a joyous occasion and is often followed by a reception for family and friends that's similar to the reception following a wedding, and calls for similar shots.

Like weddings, bar mitzvahs are often photographed by studio photographers or Uncle Harry. But, just as with wedding receptions, you may be able to get work at bar mitzvahs through personal references, as well as through caterers, florists, and printers who handle invitations for such events.

The advice offered in Chapter 7 on weddings, concerning what photographic packages to offer, what equipment to use, and how to collect your money all applies to bar mitzvahs as well.

Individual Portraits

The minister (or priest or rabbi), director of music, education director, youth director, and other members of the church or synagogue staff usually make quite a few "guest appearances" at other churches, conferences, or meetings during the year. Many occasions arise when they need photographs of themselves to use in brochures, news releases, church bulletins, and magazines. Offer to take portraits of church or synagogue officials at an appropriate location in the church and provide multiple copies so they can always have a supply to use as needed.

Sports

More and more religious groups are getting involved in sports. Some are conducting their own programs for children of members, or at least sponsoring teams in various religious leagues.

Basketball and softball are the two most active religion-related sports, with volleyball ranking a close third. Some also sponsor teams in such sports as soccer, golf, tennis, and gymnastics.

A sports director is not an uncommon position on the staff of a church or synagogue today. Make contact with him, or with the minister or rabbi. They'll want the same type of photographs that you offer to Little League and high school teams. Posing the team, and the equipment used, will be identical to methods used for Little League (see Chapter 9).

Brochures

Practically every church or synagogue is involved in a building-fund program of some type. Many of them produce elaborate brochures to show the need for increased facilities and programs; these are fund-raising pieces.

I did a twenty-four-page, 8½x11 brochure for a local church that

These two photos of the same church steeple are as different as night and day. Wouldn't either of them be great on the cover of a church bulletin? Churches and synagogues have many uses for photos and can be important customers for your freelance photography business.

was involved in a fund-raising program for an entire new complex, including a sanctuary. The piece contained photographs of just about everything that happens in a church community. Showing this brochure to other churches as a sample of my work resulted in contracts for several similar projects.

New Members

Several churches in our community feature large bulletin boards which contain portraits of each new member or family that joins. These aren't formal portraits; they're usually just quick shots made after the Sunday service.

Such a practice is a good way to help make newcomers feel at home, and to help old members recognize them on sight. Being greeted by people who know their names makes a mighty good impression on new church members.

You can usually arrange to make these photos on one or two Sundays out of the month, so you won't have something you have to do every Sunday afternoon.

Choirs

Choirs are usually very important parts of religious services, and they're almost always completely volunteer except for, perhaps, a paid director and organist. If the choir performs at activities outside the church, they'll often need a group shot for publicity.

You might also mention to the minister or rabbi that giving each choir member a color group photo would be a nice way to say thanks for a job well done.

Church-Sponsored Organizations

Most churches and synagogues also sponsor youth-related activities such as Cub Scouts, Boy Scouts, Girl Scouts, and Brownies. There are youth groups such as Methodist Youth Fellowship, the Baptist Church's Royal Ambassadors and Girls in Action, and the Jewish group Hillel. Each of these will offer picture possibilities during the course of a year. Each group elects new officers once a year. They also go on various outings, keep scrapbooks, take part in fund-raising or charity projects, select outstanding members for the year, and usually put on special programs for the congregation or the public.

Check with the youth director on these activities.

Church Directories

Church directories that contain a group photo of each member family are almost as big a business as school yearbooks. There are quite a few national companies that specialize in producing these. They have traveling photographers who'll come into the church for a week, photograph each family, and then return in about a month with proofs. The idea here is that the company will produce the directory for the church free, or at a very low price, for the privilege of being able to try to sell color photographs to all the members of the church.

While I know of some churches and synagogues that have been well pleased with their directories, I know of quite a few others who became quite unhappy with the high-pressure techniques of the people who came to show the proofs and to try to sell the photographs. In many cases they've also gotten very slow delivery of the directories and/or very poor-quality printing.

Some churches have worked with national companies on the first directory, but have worked out an arrangement with a local printer and photographer when they got ready to do a second directory several years later.

If you run into a situation like this, you may or may not want to consider it. Photographing an entire congregation can be very lucrative if the members order the photographs, but printing such a publication can be very expensive. As an individual businessman, I wouldn't want to gamble on selling enough of the photographs to offer the directory free, as the national companies do. I wouldn't mind shooting the photographs on speculation, as long as the church had a separate deal with the printer.

Each church or synagogue is really like a little separate community unto itself. You have a wide cross-section of your entire area represented there. In addition to the photographic services you can provide for the organization, you will also make many valuable contacts for other jobs among the individual members.

Chapter Nineteen

Animal Shows and Pet Portraits

(Those furry, toothy critters mean $)

Pets and animals are big business in this country. Have you ever seen the figures on how many billions of dollars we Americans spend annually on food, health products, and accessories for our animals? It's staggering! Pet owners will spend money on photography also! Are you getting any of it?

Organizations for Everything

There are organizations and shows for all kinds of horses (Arabians, quarter horses, Tennessee walkers, etc.), as well as dog and cat shows, frog jumping contests, even rat races. There are field trials for bird dogs, beagles, coonhounds, and other hunting dogs. Some folks make a living (or enjoy a luxurious leisure) following various shows and trials all across the country.

While many of these large shows have their own regular photographers who also follow the show circuit, quite a few of the local and smaller shows don't. The animal lovers who take part in these small shows, however, are just as proud of their critters and just as avid as those who pursue the activity on a national or international basis.

Winners at these local shows and photographers go together like beer and pretzels. If you have any contacts with such shows, use them! If you don't have any, get some! Local veterinarians are a good place to start. They can usually put you in touch with sponsors of the various shows and organizations.

Individual Pet Photos

Photographing individual pets is getting to be big business, also. I've done quite a few jobs in this area, and, believe me, they're never dull. Pet owners always seem to be surprised when they find a photographer who's willing to do pet portraits. Apparently many professionals refuse to do them. Yet some of the biggest orders I've ever sold were pet portraits.

My most extensive assignment in pet photography was a photo album of twelve portraits of a family cat. The album was to be one of the youngest daughter's gifts from Santa. I spent several hours with this feline at her home one morning. I'd never met such a photogenic subject in my life. Everything she did, every time she moved, seemed to be a perfect portrait opportunity. My only problem was that I shot too much film, which made the decision on the final prints very difficult for me and for the parents.

It turned out to be a beautiful idea and a beautiful job, one I was quite proud of. The little girl was thrilled, and I understand that even though she's a grown woman now, it's still one of her most cherished possessions. Wasn't that a unique gift? Recommend it to some of the cat or dog lovers you know.

I've also done portraits of a pair of Dobermans for a woman to use as a Father's Day gift for her husband, a Labrador retriever portrait to occupy a prominent place above the fireplace in a palatial mansion, and many other pictures of horses and dogs.

The most touching assignment was probably from the daughter who brought in an aged, ailing black cocker spaniel. The dog was near death, but the young woman wanted a portrait for her parents as a memento after this longtime family pet had passed on. Feeble as she was, the old dog seemed to sense what was happening. Her eyes perked up, and she even tried to raise those floppy ears for her portrait.

I've photographed parakeets, canaries, and even a pet raccoon. Like I said, it's never dull.

Besides veterinarians, your best contacts are pet shops and grooming parlors. They'll usually let you display a couple of samples and leave a stack of your business cards. Some grooming parlors will actively solicit business for you from their customers if you pay them a commission. You can make arrangements to do the portraits right at the parlor, immediately after the animal has been washed and combed or clipped. What better time? People who work at these places are also experienced animal handlers and can help you with the posing.

Speaking of Posing

Although it can be quite difficult to get an animal to sit or stand still, sometimes it's much easier to work with an animal than a human. For one thing, animals aren't self-conscious—just inquisitive.

Just like people portraits, pet portraits can be formal or informal. Here we have an informal people-pet portrait that shows a lot of love and affection.

It's usually best to have the owner along; the animal will listen to him sooner than to a stranger. Cats usually aren't much of a problem. Most of the time they'll stay where you put them, at least for a couple of minutes. Dogs will usually respond quite favorably to a toy that makes a whistling or squeaking sound. Often they'll cock their heads to one side and look in the direction the noise comes from. This is a fantastic pose. It never hurts to have a few treats in your pocket as a reward or an incentive for perhaps one more shot.

Animals trained to participate in shows are no problem; they've been taught to pose for the judges. The owner will usually know what pose is best.

Horses can be a problem, especially when they're swatting flies with their tails. Once I used masking tape to secure a horse's tail to her hind leg. About the only other thing you can do is wait until the tail is still for a moment. You'd better be ready to shoot quickly.

Poses for horses are very exacting. You can study some of the horse magazines, or visit a local show horse owner and get him to spend some time with you on proper posing. I'm sure he'd be willing to trade you some time and instruction for a few free photographs.

There may be times when you'll get requests for photographing unusual pets such as gerbils, snakes, birds, fish, etc. About the only way to handle rodents is to shoot them through glass or have the owners hold them in their hands. Naturally you'll have to shoot fish through glass, and because of personal preference, I'll shoot snakes only through glass. Your polarizing filter will help with reflections.

A word about possible dangers in photographing animals: Your best defense is common sense! Don't walk so close to a horse's back legs that he can kick you; don't pet a snarling dog; don't make any quick moves around animals—these warnings are just common sense. Let the owner handle the animal. Instruct the owner in posing and let him make the necessary adjustments. By following a few rules like these, I've avoided any problems that might pose a danger.

Equipment

My 2¼ camera and a tripod are about it for shooting animals outdoors. Flash fill is a help at times. Indoors I use the same setup for pet portraits as I do for people portraits—light bounced out of an umbrella.

It's always best to work with the camera on a tripod. That way you have both hands free to work with the animal. You can also prefocus your camera on the spot where you want the animal to be. When you get him still and on the spot, you're ready to shoot. An extension shutter-release cable can also be a help, allowing you to be several feet away from the camera and still make the exposure at just the right moment.

Packages and Pricing

I usually charge a little more for pet portraits than I do for people portraits. They usually take more time, and I usually shoot more film to make certain I've got a good selection for the customer. Often I've sold prints from more than one pose because "There were so many good poses, I couldn't decide on just one!" Boy, do I love to hear that kind of comment. You'd be surprised how many people carry photos of their pets around in their wallets just like they do photos of their children.

When working a horse or pet show, I usually offer prom sets, just as I do for pictures of athletes and dancers. If it's a large show, often I'll take two cameras: one for those who want prom sets, and one for those who prefer a single 8x10 print.

Chapter Twenty

Working with a Local Print Shop and a National Postcard Firm

(A profitable subcontract market)

Since I've also worked as a writer and as a graphic designer, I've been able to combine those two activities with my photography on many jobs. By having a working agreement with a local printer, I can offer a package deal on such things as brochures, small tabloid-type publications, booklets, catalog sheets, and catalogs.

You can do the same thing. Even if you don't know graphics—such things as layout and design—print shops do. Find one that's willing to cooperate with you, and then work out a sort of subcontractor arrangement.

Find out what the client wants, and then offer him the complete job all wrapped up in one neat price, including photography, layout and design, and printing. Once he turns it over to you, he won't have to worry about the job. When you deliver the piece, it will be ready to use.

The one area in which I don't work with local printers is color postcards. I find I get much better results at much cheaper prices from national firms that specialize in this type of color printing, but we'll discuss this a little later.

Print Shops as a Job Source

Printers are a good source of contacts, also. They have customers all the time who need quick photos to go in their printed pieces. Often customers call a printer and ask him to recommend a photographer for other jobs, as well.

Printers can also be a source of wedding jobs for you. Most of them sell wedding invitations. You'd be surprised how many tradespeople such as these a prospective bride will ask for recommendations of wedding photographers. Ask the printer to let you display several wedding photographs in the shop and put a couple of bridal portraits in the book of wedding invitation samples. Have your name and "Wedding Photographer" stamped in gold on the front of each photo. The printer can handle this for you. You might even make up a small portfolio of your work and leave it at the shop, so the printer can show samples of your work to any prospective clients.

Of course, you should make the same effort to gain customers for the printer. If you're working on a brochure for a company and happen to hear them discuss getting a new letterhead or ordering more bill forms, suggest they contact your printer. Helping each other get more work is a two-way street.

Don't Skimp on Your Own Printing

Another good thing about working with a printer is that you can usually get a discount on your own printing needs. That way you can afford a better grade of paper or a more distinctive letterhead or business card.

Remember, your first contact with potential customers is most often through printing (you'll tell your clients this to sell them package deals). What does your printing tell future clients about you? This is the same question you'll be raising with clients who are interested in printing/photo package deals.

Don't skimp! Have printed pieces that you can be proud of, and they'll give *a good first impression* to your clients (no pun intended!).

Postcards

Practically all resort-related businesses—hotels and motels, large restaurants, golf courses, tennis clubs, amusement parks, fishing piers, and charter boats—as well as many regular businesses and industries, use color postcards and brochures for promotion. This represents a very handsome market for the freelance photographer because he can make money in two ways: by taking the color slide or photograph used for the card or brochure, and by selling the card or brochure order, which he then subcontracts to a national firm that specializes in such items. There are quite a few of these postcard firms throughout the nation, and at the end of this chapter I'll list several with which I've dealt. By the way, the same companies produce color brochures at reasonable prices.

Unlikely Users of Postcards. Besides some of the obvious users of postcards, like resorts and amusement facilities, I've sold orders to some businesses you'd never think would have any use for them.

One of these was a poultry farm which shipped baby chicks through the mail. They used a color postcard with a photo of baby

Organizations like the Florence (South Carolina) Air and Missile Museum use many different postcards of their exhibits. When you contract to provide a firm with postcards, you make money off the photography and also get a commission for selling the card order. How's that for a double money-maker?

chicks to acknowledge customer orders. A trucking firm ordered post-cards to announce a new fleet of eighteen-wheelers that they were put-ting on the road. A building contractor had a postcard made up, featur-ing four of his latest commercial buildings, and mailed it to prospective clients throughout the state. A fishing tackle manufacturer used color postcards to announce a new lure. He mailed the cards to fishing tourna-ment participants from a list that he'd accumulated over the years.

You never know where you might sell a postcard order. Just make it a point to ask for the business.

Instruction Booklet. Most of these national postcard firms have an in-struction booklet that gives the photographer all the technical informa-tion he needs in order to enter the postcard market. These booklets also have helpful information on how to sell orders, what types of businesses use postcards most often, and how to approach prospective clients. The technical information includes: what type of slides or color photographs they can use, how to take the photograph, how to design the card or brochure, how to fill out the order form, and much more.

In addition to providing order forms and materials, the firms also give you a price list and samples of every service they offer. These services usually include photo business cards, postcards, brochures of various sizes, and catalog sheets. The price list will give the total cost of the order, as well as a deposit the customer must pay you at the time the order is taken. This deposit usually represents the photographer's com-mission for selling the order. It allows you to get your money in advance, so you won't have to wait until the cards are printed and delivered.

Special Requirements and Abilities. These national firms that specialize in color postcards and color brochures can give much cheaper prices, and usually better work, on these particular types of jobs than local printers, because they're set up to handle these orders exclusively.

While sometimes they require a 4x5 as the minimum size of color transparency for some large cards and brochures, most will accept 2¼x2¼ or 2¼x2¾, and some will even work from 35mm. Some firms will work from color prints; some will not. As in most other applications, you can expect better-quality work from the larger-sized slides or negatives. If they work from prints, they should be 8x10.

These firms also have outstanding airbrush artists, who can help spruce up otherwise so-so photographs. Telephone and power lines and poles are usually a bother in trying to get a decent photograph of a building. The artist can remove these completely from your photograph. Did you have a clear, blue sky as a background on a particular shot? Wouldn't it be a lot better if there had been a few fluffy white clouds? The artist can add these for you with no trouble at all. Of course, there's usually an extra charge for this type of work, but it's nominal and can be well worth the price.

Credit Line. There's a line of print in the center of the message side of the card where a photographer can add his own credit line for the photography and the card. Most companies, while they ship the finished order directly to the customer, are quite nice about sending the original artwork and several samples of each job back to the photographer for his use. It always helps to be able to show a potential customer a high-quality color postcard with your credit line printed on it.

Also, whether the customer calls you or goes directly to the card manufacturer for reprint orders, you get a commission on these reprint sales as well. Reprint orders, over the years, can account for a nice profit several times from just one job.

Some Postcard Firms.

> Dynacolor Graphics, Inc.
> 1182 N.W. 159th Dr.
> Miami FL 33169
>
> McGrew Color Graphics
> Box 19716
> Kansas City MO 64141

Again I remind you that if a firm isn't listed here, it doesn't mean that I wouldn't recommend them; it just means that I've probably never tried them.

Send to these companies for your sales kit, and then decide from their samples, price list, and instruction booklet which one you want to use.

Chapter Twenty-one

Slide Shows

(Cheaper than movies but just as effective)

Some people think of slide shows as cheap movies. I don't! For one thing, they don't move. But they *are* much cheaper to produce than motion pictures, and often they do just as effective a job.

Slide presentations can be quite simple or quite complicated. The audio portion can consist of a speaker who talks about each slide as he flashes it on the screen. There can also be a prerecorded narration sound-synced with each slide, or you can have a multiscreen and multi-image show made up of several synchronized slide projectors with accompanying recorded narration, music, and appropriate sound effects.

Sell to the Business Community

Just about every business and industry can use some type of slide presentation if they're sold on the idea of what it can produce for them.

Slide shows can be effective as training aids for personnel—from secretaries and other office workers to assembly line workers and advanced electronic technicians.

A slide presentation can sell a product to a large or medium-sized group of people or to an individual executive in his office. With modern, small, portable, self-contained rear-screen projectors, you can set up a slide presentation right on the corner of the busy executive's desk—and not even have to turn the lights off or shade the windows.

Slide presentations are an effective public relations tool for the firm that needs to get its story across to the general public. They can be used for recruiting students, personnel, or customers.

How many firms can you think of right now who could benefit from an effective slide presentation? Then what are you doing sitting there? Get out and sell, man—sell!

A slide show is a natural for a taxidermist to use in promoting his business. It could begin with a customer bringing in an animal to be mounted, and show each step in progress to the finished job. Just about any business could use a slide show for promotion, selling, training, or a multitude of public relations activities.

Sell Slide Shows with Slide Shows. When you visit a business executive to sell him a slide presentation, what could be more impressive than to do it with your own slide presentation?

If you can't afford to buy one of the small, self-contained projection units, some camera stores will rent them for a moderate fee. If you help sell your customer on a particular unit to go with the slide show you're going to do for him, the camera store might work with you by providing a projector for your use at no charge, or selling you one at their cost.

If you do an effective job of selling the executive your services with a slide presentation, he'll be convinced that his salespeople can do the same type of job on their clients with the slide show you produce for him.

Community and Nonprofit Groups

While you were making a list of all the firms that could benefit from a slide presentation, did you include yourself? Why not? You're a photographer! Can you think of a better way to sell your services and use your own work to do it? Let me give you a couple of examples of the ways I've used slide shows.

In Chapter 17, Garden Clubs, I told you about those program chairmen who're always looking for a program. Well, that doesn't stop with garden clubs. How many civic clubs are there in your town? How about churches, men's fellowship groups or clubs, women's circle meetings? Business organizations, social clubs, professional fraternities— they all have meetings, and they all need programs.

You could do a slide presentation on flower arranging or how to take pictures for the garden clubs. A presentation on how to decorate a home or office with photographs would be appropriate for both men's and women's groups. Tips on photographing children would make a good program anywhere. Photography as an effective communications tool for business and industry is a great subject for executives. How to photograph your pet or tips on making home slide shows or movies more enjoyable would be fine for general groups. How to use photography in selling would be of interest to all civic clubs that are made up of businessmen and women.

The list is endless, and I don't expect you to do them all, but surely there are some that appeal to you. You've probably already got quite a few slides on hand that would be appropriate for some of these shows. Now you just have to get the script done!

Some additional subjects that I've worked up into slide shows include: travel photography, aerial scenes of your hometown (local businesses, industry, schools, highway systems, etc.), a visit to a local zoo, how to take pictures of your fishing trip. There are so many possibilities that would make interesting programs and give your own career a boost at the same time.

Equipment

Your 35mm camera and your strobes and umbrellas will take care of most of your assignments. A wide-angle lens is probably the next most important piece of equipment for shooting, and occasionally you may have need for a moderate telephoto.

Another nice thing to have is some type of light-table to view your slides. One of those little lighted viewers that includes a magnifying glass is fine for looking at one slide at a time. But when putting together a slide show, you need a large lighted area where you can spread out many slides at the same time. You can purchase one of these for just a few dollars. They're made out of a piece of cardboard, which can be folded to make a box covered on one side by a piece of plastic that holds rows of slides. This box is lined with a reflective material and has a bare light bulb stuck through a hole in the side. You can also buy more expensive ones that are made of metal and have frosted glass rather than plastic viewing areas.

It's not difficult to make your own, sized to hold any number of slides you desire, by nailing four pieces of wood together to form a rectangle. Inside the rectangle, about one-half to one inch from the top, nail small strips of wood to support a piece of frosted glass or plastic (which you can have cut to size). Insert a light bulb for your light source, and you're in business.

How to Start

There are two essentials of any good slide presentation: First, you need a good script; second, you need good slides.

The script should come first. It's the road map you'll follow for the visual part of the presentation. If you can write the script as well as produce the slides, so much the better. Again, you get paid for two jobs instead of one. Whether you write the script or not, insist that you have it in hand and that you understand its purpose before you go out and start shooting.

Remember also that *good* slides mean more than proper exposure, balanced lighting, and sharp focus. Each shot must tell a vital part of the overall story you're presenting. It must relate to the overall sequence. Always keep in mind that you're trying to *tell a story*.

The slide show might be about the life and loves of a blast furnace, or about a manufacturing process for refrigerators, but it's still a story that must be told in a logical sequence. You can't jump around from one place to another or one part of the process to another.

If you're a little weak in your writing skills, most colleges and universities offer courses which can be of immense help. Community schools have writing courses from time to time, and there are also a few excellent correspondence courses available to help you.

Some Are Quite Involved

The most comprehensive slide show I've ever done was on the subject of how to build a house. It ended up with more than five hundred slides in its finished form and told the story in detail, beginning with clearing the lot and digging and laying the foundation, continuing right on up through plumbing, electrical work, roofing, and, finally, painting.

This particular presentation was used by technical and vocational schools in their training courses for the various building trades.

The script was written and the slides arranged in such a manner that instructors could show the entire presentation and then go back and pull out the individual sections for more detailed study for their groups—whether they were carpenters, plumbers, electricians, bricklayers, or whatever.

Rather than drag out the shooting over the entire time it took to build one particular house, I found a residential contractor who had several projects going at the same time, all in different phases of construction. By having so many houses to work with, I was able to shoot the complete job in a period of two to three weeks.

Of course, I first wrote the script. It took another two or three weeks to interview all the people involved in building a house and to learn the sequence of tasks and the interrelationship of all the different subcontractors.

When you stop to think that a slide show of this type can be used in eight or ten different schools, thus requiring many duplicate sets of slides, the few weeks I spent were very well rewarded.

Chapter Twenty-two

Marinas

(If it floats, they want a photo of it)

Most people can't afford the boats they buy. Since they've had to struggle and save for years in order to be able to purchase them, they're proud of their crafts.

I've sold lots of boat photographs—from powerboats, racing boats, and small fishing outfits to large cruisers, pontoon boats, and sailboats of all sizes. Some families have even used their boats as settings for family portraits and Christmas cards.

Equipment

You won't need any special equipment to photograph boats. As long as your camera has a shutter speed of at least 1/500 second, you'll be okay. A polarizing filter would be good to help reduce reflections from the water and from shiny boat surfaces.

If you're clumsy, one of those waterproof camera pouches might save your photo equipment from a dunking. If you feel the need for one of these pouches, then I'd also invest in a life jacket!

Boat Picture Day

If you live on the coast or near an inland lake or reservoir that has a lot of recreational activity, contact a couple of local marinas. Suggest to them the possibility of sponsoring a "picture day" for people who have purchased boats from them or who store boats at the marina.

You can set up on the end of the dock and just have the owners file by. The marina owner may want to pick up the tab for the photos as a public relations gesture, or pick up a part of it and offer the photos to his customers at a nominal price.

Don't go near the water—unless you're looking for extra income. This picture was for a newspaper advertisement.

As a part of the deal, get the marina owner to include your name in the newspaper, radio, and television advertising of the event.

Boating Clubs

There are sailboat clubs, boat camping clubs, canoe clubs, and fishing clubs of all kinds, all made up of people who are proud of their boats. Contact them and try to arrange the same kind of picture day.

You can offer prom sets or single 8x10s on all these activities. Regardless of what you offer, you'll more than likely get some reprint orders also.

You can find out about the various types of clubs in your area from boat dealers and marinas.

Action Shots

Many boat owners will want action shots of their rigs, especially sailboats. A sailboat without its sails up and full isn't very picturesque, and when those sails are full, it's going to be moving!

Powerboats can also be very impressive in action, especially those that ride on top of the water or throw a rooster tail of spray from their props.

You can shoot these action photos from a pier if it's in deep enough water. You'll probably have to pan your camera as the boat passes by.

If you're shooting from another boat, try to arrange for one that's large and stable; something like a cruiser is great, or perhaps a pontoon boat. If you can get a little more elevation above the water than the boat you're shooting, you'll be in good shape.

Some extensive jobs, such as shooting boats for a manufacturer's catalog, may dictate hiring a truck with a cherry picker (one of those plastic buckets that elevate people to work on things like power lines) to hold you up and out over the water. A cruiser with a tall flying bridge will also work well.

If there are boat manufacturers in your area, be sure to check with them. They all publish annual catalogs, as well as catalog sheets and brochures, and they use lots of photos.

Marinas Advertise, Too

The marina owner might also want some action shots of some of the boats in his inventory for advertising purposes. Or he may need a slide show of the different lines and types he stocks for showing to groups of potential customers. Photos of his dock spaces or dry storage facilities can also be helpful sales aids.

Aerial photos of marinas are always dramatic and make good advertising illustrations (see Chapter 12, on aerial photography). I did an aerial shot for a marina that was used in its Yellow Pages advertising for years, as well as on its calendars. Aerial shots are also great for brochures. Some marinas use large aerial photos or sets of aerials on their walls, so they can show newcomers or new boat owners how to get around without getting lost.

Fishing Tournaments

Many marinas are sites for local fishing tournaments several times a year. At the end of a day of competition, contestants return to the marina to weigh in their catches and determine the winners.

If a fisherman likes catching a big fish more than anything, his second biggest thrill is having his photograph taken showing that fish off. Combine this with the fact that he just won a trophy and some cash by catching that fish, and you know darn well you've just made a sale if you're there with your camera.

Be sure and get your money on the spot! He may catch an even bigger fish and win an even bigger trophy the next week, before you've had time to deliver the photograph.

People are proud of their boats. Take advantage of this fact, and you might make enough money off the resulting photographs to buy your own boat!

Chapter Twenty-three

Conventions and Meetings

(Big meetings mean big bucks)

Even if your town isn't large enough to attract conventions, there are many opportunities available for group photographs of meetings and photos of individual activities that go along with such get-togethers.

Class Reunions

High school and college class reunions are meetings that occur almost everywhere. Each school usually has at least one group a year who come back to remember the good old times and see how everybody else has changed. Here's a chance for you to sell a bunch of prints from just one shot. Surely they'll all want a photo of the gang.

Collect your money in advance for this group shot, and mail the photos out to each person. Be sure to add your costs for postage and envelopes into the price.

You can find out which classes are having reunions and who's in charge of organizing these reunions by checking with the school or college alumni or alumnae office.

Civic Clubs

Each civic club usually has at least two events during the year to which the members invite their wives or husbands, and many also have another event for the family, which includes children.

Most meetings that feature special speakers are also good opportunities for photos.

Clubs need photographs of new officers after each annual election. In addition to photos for news releases, most clubs also need pictures for their scrapbooks of community and club activities.

If you live in a larger town, the chamber of commerce should have a list of all civic clubs in the area and their officers. In smaller towns, you can check out the larger restaurants. They'll have signs listing the clubs that meet there and the meeting dates.

Company Picnics

Many large businesses and industries have one or two annual outings for employees and their families, such as company picnics or Christmas parties. These always call for a lot of photos: family groups having a good time, various contest and game winners, Santa giving out presents, etc.

Photos are also used for the company newspaper or magazine and are posted on bulletin boards or given to the individuals involved.

Check with the personnel or public relations department. While some of these firms have staff photographers, most of them don't. While you're there, also inquire about doing work on a regular basis for any company publications. You never know!

Masons, Shriners, Eastern Star

Fraternal organizations always have photos taken of their new officers and usually of their new members.

These organizations also have many special events during the year, such as dances, picnics, parades, and special benefits; each is a photo possibility.

Shriners, in particular, have special parade units that feature marching groups, bands, motorcycle or miniature car units, and old buses or hearses fancifully decorated; all are picture possibilities. The Shriners usually like to have posed shots of these various units to use for publicity purposes, as well as action shots taken while the units are actually performing in parades, at ball games, etc.

Conventions

The local chamber of commerce or the sales office of a hotel is an excellent source for determining what conventions or large meetings are scheduled for your city. It will also be able to provide you with the name and address of the person in charge of setting up the event for the organization involved.

Conventions are great money-makers for freelancers. Not only are there official shots for the sponsors of the meeting, but also photos for individuals who want mementos of the occasion. Usually each session of the convention will mean photographs of the speaker, the head table, and special award presentations and candid shots of the delegates.

In addition to business meetings, there are beauty contests, dances, exhibits, demonstrations, hospitality rooms and displays, door prize awards, and many other scenes and events.

Practically every organization that's large enough to put on a convention has a publication that uses lots of photographs. They also send photos out with news releases.

A Time-Consuming but Lucrative Job. Working a convention will require a good deal of your time, with either waits at the hotel between activities or two or three trips back and forth a day between home and headquarters (if you live close enough). But the amount of money you'll make from even a small meeting of this type can be well worth your time. I don't believe I've ever had a convention job, even a small one, that brought in less than $100. If you land a large meeting, you can expect to hit the $500-to-$1,000 range.

Need for Quick Prints. I have worked with convention groups that required the photographer to process and proof each day's shots overnight and have them on display the next morning. Prints are numbered so that delegates can order copies of the photographs they want sent to them. While this plan makes for some hectic shooting and darkroom work, the reward is worth all the hassle. You'll sell a lot more prints if delegates can see them shortly after they're taken and while people are still caught up in the enthusiasm of the convention.

This is one occasion where a stabilization processor (discussed in Chapter 3, on darkrooms) would come in mighty handy. With it, plus a portable enlarger, some tanks and reels for processing film, and a safelight, you could set up a darkroom right in the bathroom of one of the hotel rooms. Convention directors usually rent a couple of extra rooms to work out of, so there'd be no extra charge involved for you.

With this type of operation, you could put your waiting time between meetings and other activities to good use, processing your film and making prints. If the job were large enough, you could have someone else in the family or a part-time associate go along to do the darkroom work.

These stabilization prints would also be quite handy for anyone connected with the convention who had to have prints to take with him when he left the meeting—for example, a newspaper reporter or editor or a salesperson who needs rush prints of a new piece of equipment or merchandise he saw at the convention. The convention director also may need to send rush prints out to newspapers or other trade magazines. In these circumstances, a stabilization processor could be worth its weight in gold.

Trade Shows. If the meeting has an accompanying trade show or exhibition, you can usually sell color shots of each display to the individual exhibitor. Some exhibitors will try to hire you for the duration of the show to take a photo of each important customer or client who stops by their booths. If they want you badly enough, bring in another photographer to help out; one of you can stay at this booth and the other handle the regular convention business.

About Your Pay. Some conventions have set budgets for photographs, and they won't exceed them. Nevertheless, they'll usually ask you to give them bids on how much you'll charge them to do the jobs.

Of course, in order to come to a realistic figure, you'll have to take into account many factors, including how many photographs they'll want, how much time is going to be involved, and whether or not you're going to have to hire someone to help you with the coverage. Never start out with a low quote. You can always come down; you can never go up in price.

Of course, any money you may make on prints sold to convention delegates, exhibitors, etc., won't be included in this price. The extras are all yours. You're quoting only on work for the sponsors of the event, unless they want to pay for all the photographs, including those mentioned above.

Even when a convention director has given you a set number of photographs to shoot for a set price, if you see something that's interesting and important but isn't on your list, shoot it anyway. The small investment in film and prints will pay off in most cases, because you'll often find a buyer for these extra shots at the convention.

Chapter Twenty-four

Legal Photography

(Grab your camera—here comes the judge)

You can make good money doing photography for lawyers, but if you're squeamish or don't want to get your trousers dirty, you'd better stay away from this aspect of the business.

Lawyers are liable to have you crawling under wrecked automobiles and trucks, inside tanks, under houses, or in the walls and attics of homes and commercial businesses; wading in flooded basements; or photographing traffic while you're standing in the middle of a busy intersection. You name it, and they'll probably need it at one time or another.

Subjects for your portrait lens will most likely be burn victims, wreck victims, fight victims, and other accident victims. You'll be training your camera on some pretty gruesome-looking scars, disfigurements, and wounds.

You might be working in a hospital room, emergency room, doctor's office, lawyer's office, or some other location—and heaven only knows where that location could be, or in what type of weather or under what type of conditions you'll be working.

It's not for the faint of heart or stomach, but the pay is tops. There are probably many lawyers in your town. You can start to work today, if you want to.

How to Get the Jobs

There are three ways to make your contacts: by a personal visit to the lawyer's office (he's usually out or busy with a client), by letter, or by telephone. I've used all three, but have gotten best results by sending a letter first, followed up by a phone call.

Lawyers are busy people, and you won't get much of their time.

Always have your sales pitch perfected and be ready to show samples of your work.

The assignments you'll be getting usually won't be the kind that can wait. If a lawyer tells you he has to have a photo made right now, it's for a good reason. Don't turn him down unless you absolutely must. If you do, you'll probably lose a client.

Equipment

You won't need any special equipment for legal photography, but it's always best to use at least a 2¼ camera if possible. You never know when you'll be called on to enlarge your photographs up to 20x24 inches, or even bigger, for use as evidence in court. This is especially true in the case of injuries to people, which may leave scars or disfigurement. When photographs of a person are enlarged to more than life size, even a small scar is quite dramatic.

Records Are Important

More so than in any other type of photography, accurate records here are a *MUST!* You'll be asked to write on the back of each photograph the time and date it was made, a statement that it was personally taken and processed by you (if someone else did the processing, state who did), the location where it was taken, and your signature.

The above information should be recorded on your negative file for that particular job, as well. Also make a notation of what the weather conditions were. And for goodness' sake, *don't lose the negatives!*

Remember, retouching legal photographic negatives or prints is strictly a no-no! Don't ever try to make even the slightest correction or touch-up. A photo for legal purposes isn't expected to be a work of art, just an accurate record of what happened, where it happened, or the results it left.

Of course, you realize that if you intentionally alter a photograph to try to show something that isn't there, or cover up something that is, you're breaking the law. Participating in conspiracy or committing perjury and getting caught aren't worth any amount of money.

Accurate Records

Why keep accurate records? Because you could well be called on to testify in court, unless the case is settled before it gets there.

You'll be expected to take your negatives and your records to court with you. Under oath, you'll be asked to examine each photograph, state that you took it, and tell under whose direction and under what conditions you took it, what the weather was like, and so on.

You'll know that it's the photograph you took and turned over to the lawyer because it will have your information and signature recorded on the back of it. When you're on the stand and they hand you the photograph to examine, be sure you turn it over and look at it to see if your signature is there before you state for the record that it's your photograph! This small action will make your testimony more believable and your lawyer-client happy.

You should get paid for your time spent in court. If the lawyer forgets to mention it, ask him about it—*before you testify,* not after.

Fees

Your work is important, so charge for it! As with every other job, it's best to work out your charges in advance, but when doing legal work, start higher than you would on an ordinary job. And don't be surprised if you find out later that the lawyer marked your charges up some more before the client got the bill.

I got a call one night to travel to a town some twenty-five miles away. There was a wrecked pickup truck on a lot there that would probably be moved to an undisclosed location the next day. The lawyer needed a photograph of the inside of the left front wheel for legal purposes. I got there in the rain and had to crawl through a hole in the fence and lie on the wet ground under the truck to shoot. I took two photographs and charged the lawyer $175.

He was extremely happy. Those two photographs were directly responsible for proving that a nut had never been placed on a bolt on this new truck; the truck was wrecked because of this oversight. The lawyer won the case in court for his client and collected many thousands of dollars in this suit.

Finally, don't forget to charge for your mileage and travel time, in addition to your fee for the photographs!

What to Shoot

Often a lawyer will tell you exactly what he wants, but there will be times when you'll be on the scene alone and will have to use your best judgment as to the angles, distance, and number of shots that will allow the best possible presentation of the case.

On automobile wreck scenes, for instance, if there are any skid marks on the pavement which indicate how far the vehicle traveled after the brakes were applied, you'll certainly want to shoot these. If the automobile or automobiles are still on the scene, you'll want to shoot them from several different angles. Should there happen to be a liquor bottle at the scene, you'll want a shot of that—*but do not touch anything.* If the liquor bottle is half covered by a floor mat, *do not* pull the mat

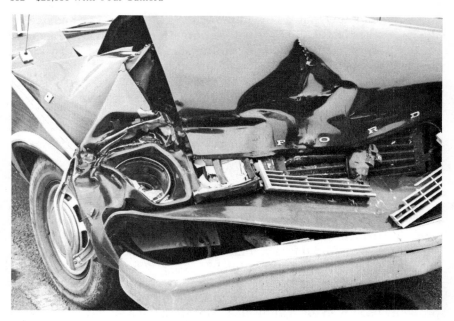

Often in legal photography you'll have to use your own judgment on
what the lawyer needs. In shooting auto wrecks, always get a shot to
show the point of impact. If, as in the second photo, it appears that
someone's head or a missile of some kind might have hit the wind-
shield, you'll certainly want to shoot that.

aside to show the bottle better. The same holds true for drugs, firearms, or anything else in the vehicle that may be a potential piece of evidence. Never arrange or rearrange any potential evidence at the scene of an accident or a crime.

The best rule for any legal photography is to shoot more shots than you think you're going to need. Remember, film costs are always the cheapest part of the job. Something that might seem insignificant to you might be very important to the lawyer. If you don't think it will be necessary to print up large photographs of everything you shoot, give the lawyer a proof sheet and let him decide what he needs.

If the members of any profession in your town outnumber real estate agents, they're probably lawyers. There aren't many cases a lawyer handles in which he doesn't need photographs, or wouldn't use them if they were available. I've known photographers who more or less specialized in this type of work, earning up to a third or a half of their photographic income from it.

A half dozen lawyers as clients could put you a good way down the road toward that $25,000 figure.

Chapter Twenty-five

Passport and Application Photos

(These you can call mug shots)

Passport and application photos—commonly referred to as mug shots—have gotten to be big business, even though they're tiny photographs.

Contrary to popular belief, you don't have to have an established studio in order to get into this area of the profession. All you need is a 2¼ camera, one umbrella and strobe unit, two light stands, and a background. Since all of this equipment is quite portable, you can readily set it up in your living room or den or take it on location.

I was once contacted by a local high school French club, which was planning a summer trip abroad. All the members and sponsors who were going to make the trip needed passports, which meant that they each needed passport photographs. Two identical photographs are required with the passport application.

Rather than face the prospect of having some seventy-five students trekking through my home, I made arrangements to set up at the school and do all the passport photos during one afternoon. That one job made my house payments for a couple of months.

If people getting passports intend to drive in a foreign country, they also need to apply for international driver's licenses. Those require additional photos.

Some countries require visas, which mean more photographs; the exact number needed varies from country to country.

I recall one family of five who were going to Saudi Arabia. The husband was being transferred there by his employer, a construction company, and the entire family was going along. The company ordered them to have twenty passport-type photos to take with them—twenty per person! I don't know what all of them were used for, but I was happy to oblige.

Another time a real estate agent called and needed mug shots of each of his twenty-five salespeople for a newspaper ad. I loaded everything in the car, set up in his office, made twenty-five photographs, and was back home in an hour and a half.

These little photos can mean big money!

A Simple Setup

Once again, just as in dance school photography, place your single umbrella high and directly behind the camera. The background is no problem. Several companies make portable canvas backgrounds, which are quite easily held up by one light stand. If you can't afford one of these, go to a department store and buy the largest old-fashioned window shade you can find—either white, off-white, or cream. Run a wire from one end of the shade to the other and use this wire to attach the shade to your light stand. Then roll out as much window shade as you need for your background. When you're through, roll it up again. It'll store in a mighty small space.

While most passport and application work is still black-and-white, passports will now accept color, and a few applications specify color. Whether black-and-white or color, they all require a light background. As stated, I use a white, an off-white, or a cream background for black-and-white. For color I generally use light blue or light green.

If you can't afford even a window-shade background—or can't find one in a light pastel for color work—you can always cut off a piece of roll-paper background and tape it to a wall. In emergencies, I've used the wall itself as the background, provided it was light colored (no textured or patterned wallpaper), and I could avoid such things as light-switch plates, thermostats, and heat vents.

One more thing: Make sure you allow yourself enough room and enough background to be able to place the subject at least three feet away from it. Any closer, and you'll probably end up with some irritating shadows.

Special Camera

If you get into passport business in a big way, you might want to consider a special camera just for this type of work. Polaroid makes two good ones called "Mini-Portrait" cameras. One model delivers two identical photos (it has two lenses) on a sheet of 4x5 Polaroid film, either black-and-white or color. (Instant color film is approved for passport photos.) The other camera delivers four identical photos (it has four lenses) on one sheet of 4x5 film. For lighting you can use one umbrella, or there's a flash shoe so you can mount your strobe directly on the camera. But there are fewer shadows and no red eyes to worry about if you use your umbrella.

Passport and application photos may be little pictures, but they can mean big money. Cameras like the Polaroid Mini-Portrait are ideal for this kind of work because they give you two identical photos on one sheet of 4x5 film. Another model of the camera gives you four identical photos on the same 4x5 sheet.

Another advantage of these special Mini-Portrait cameras is that they have a little plastic lens cap to cover each lens. If your customer doesn't need identical photos, you can leave one lens covered, shoot a pose, switch caps on the lenses, shoot another—and give them two poses on the same sheet of film. In the case of the camera with four lenses, you can give them four different poses, all on one sheet of film.

These cameras are prefocused; you can't adjust the focus. If you're going to photograph more than one person in the same picture, you'll need an auxiliary lens, which is available from Polaroid.

There are several other firms offering cameras of this type; most of them use the Polaroid back.

The reason you can't use just any Polaroid camera for passport photos is the requirement of two *identical* photos. This means that you cannot take two separate photos and use them. The two photos have to be taken together, as on the Mini-Portrait camera with two lenses, or be printed from the same negative with regular film.

With the Mini-Portrait cameras, you'll also have the capability of handling identification photo assignments, such as for ID cards for schools or industry.

Advantages of the Passport Freelancer

Your completely portable setup and your willingness to go on location are advantages over the studio photographer who's only willing to do such photography in the studio. Point out to potential clients that it will cost them more money for an employee to have to leave work, drive to the studio, then return to the job, than if you set up on the premises. Then, the employee can probably have his photograph taken and be back at work in less than five minutes.

Being able to deliver passport and application photos immediately with the Mini-Portrait camera is also a distinct advantage. Most people who need this type of photo usually forget about or put them off to the very last minute.

For instance, it usually takes two weeks to have a passport application processed and get the passport back. You can't even submit the application without the photos. Most people who're going overseas remember fifteen days before they're leaving that they need photos for their passports.

Application Photos

Many firms require wallet-size photos for applications—although sometimes you will get strange size requests.

In addition to being used for applications, wallet-size photos are also required for many other things. State agencies which issue various licenses require these photographs. In our state these include licenses for such people as registered nurses, cosmetologists, barbers, and real estate agents.

Persons applying for citizenship in this country must file photos with their papers; aliens are required to be photographed once a year and submit those photos with their alien report forms.

People who need these photographs will always have instruction sheets, or notations on their applications as to exactly what size and how many copies are required. If someone just asks you for a passport photo or a passport-type photo, always make sure you find out just what's required before you go to the trouble of shooting and printing them up.

Some government agencies will have quite sticky requirements, such as: ". . . exactly one and one-fourth inch from top of head to bottom of chin," or "Leave a one-half-inch white strip at bottom for applicant's signature."

Most people don't read their forms or requirements too closely. It's always best to have them bring the actual instructions and let you read them. If you don't give them what they need, you'll just have to shoot the job over again, or at least reprint it.

No RC Paper

Don't use RC paper for passport or application photos. In most cases, the applicant will have to sign the photo, and you can't write on such glossy stock.

What I usually do is use glossy paper but not gloss it on the dryer. If it's still hard to write on, just rub the space where they'll sign with a pencil eraser. Then they can write on it with no trouble.

Don't use double-weight paper, either, or a paper with any kind of pattern or texture to it. These are not acceptable for passport photos.

Regular single-weight, glossy paper, dried with the emulsion side out—toward the curtain—is always the safest bet for any of these photos.

Passports from the Post Office

Except in large cities—Washington, New York, Miami, Los Angeles, and others of that size—passports are usually issued at the main post office. They will provide you with a sheet that lists the exact requirements for passport photos; the requirements do change from time to time. It's best to check before you start shooting to find out exactly what's acceptable.

And when a client asks for passport photos—unless you know for sure that he is talking about a U.S. passport—be sure and ask what country it's for. I live in a university town, and I have foreign clients all the time. Would you believe that requirements for passport photos—size and number—are different for every country? The most common ones I get, other than American, are for Canada, England, and France, but I have had customers from countries I'd never even heard of. In that case, don't try to decipher the requirements yourself. You'll have to depend on the customer to translate!

Chapter Twenty-six

Copy Work

(Money from the past)

Most people have old photographs they'd like copied, but they usually stick these photos in a drawer and forget about them. If you can get folks to pull them out, you can make some good money.

I'm not talking about restoration of old photographs—fixing up cracks and torn spots or replacing somebody's face—we'll cover that later in the chapter. Now, I'm talking about straight copy work—taking photos of existing photos.

Equipment

Copy work isn't difficult. You've got to have a flat surface to work on, either horizontal or vertical. My primary copy board is one of those two-sided easels that they use in kindergarten. It has a couple of clips on it to hold the paper in place for the youngsters. I use the clips if what I'm copying has a wide enough margin that the clips won't be in the printing area of the negative. If the margin is narrow, then I use double-sided Scotch tape, or roll up a small piece of masking tape (so that it's double-sided) and use that to hold whatever I'm copying in place.

This type of copy board is also good for making title slides for slide presentations, copying artwork (which we'll talk about later), copying old documents, and a lot of other uses.

If you don't have one of these easels, use a heavy piece of cardboard. Nail it to a tree or lay it flat on the ground. This way you can just lay the photograph to be copied on it and use your camera on a tripod.

I do a lot of my copy work outdoors, because the lighting is so much easier. Don't work in the direct sunlight; open shade is better, and you don't have to worry about shadows.

My Mamiya C330, with its long bellows, is an excellent camera

An inexpensive kindergarten finger-paint easel makes a great copy board for reproducing old photographs or documents. I do most of my copy work outside in open shade rather than fiddle with lights indoors.

for copy work. The normal lens is usually quite sufficient. If you're copying indoors at relatively low shutter speeds, a shutter-release cable will keep you from moving the camera when you trip the shutter. Naturally, you'll have your camera on the tripod.

Pricing

This is one area where I usually charge by the photograph. Making a copy of another photo is usually something that can be done very quickly; therefore, your rate for an hour, or even a half hour, would be far too much to charge.

A Word of Caution

If someone ever brings you a legal document to copy, better check first to make sure it's lawful to make a copy of that particular item. There are some documents that cannot be copied. Some librarians know what can be copied and what can't. You might also check with the clerk at your local courthouse, or an attorney.

It should go without saying, but I'll say it anyway: Never copy any material that's covered by copyright law.

Also, never copy a registered trademark. Some studios will stamp their names or trademarks on the front of photos in gold. Believe it or not, I've had people bring me portraits they've had made at other studios, with the studio name on the print. I've also had them bring me proofs they had shot at studios. They wanted me to copy these photographs and make extra prints for them because that was cheaper than buying prints from the studio. Needless to say, I never have. I don't actually know the legalities of this, but it certainly isn't ethical.

Restorations

Surely you've had someone ask you about an old photograph that is really in decrepit condition. I've had people bring me photos with half the emulsion missing because it stuck to the glass when they tried to take them out of old frames; old glass plates that were broken; photos where half of someone's face, or a hand or a foot, was missing—terrible images, which clients wanted restored for sentimental or other reasons.

I've had people bring me an old photo of an uncle or grandfather wearing a pair of overalls and ask me to dress him in a suit and tie!

Don't laugh! It can be done very easily. All you have to do is collect your money, put the old photo in the mail, and wait for a beautiful job to come back for you to deliver.

There are quite a few firms across the nation that do this type of restoration work. One you might want to check with is Venetian Arts, Inc., Box 575, Venice, FL 33595. They have brochures on their services, which they'll be glad to send if you write and ask for them.

Airbrush artists are masters at restoring old photos. The work is done in watercolor or oils, and you can specify all colors including the shade of complexion you want and color of clothes (they'll be happy to change the clothes as you direct). They'll open closed eyes, add missing body parts—just about anything you want done.

The process they use doesn't actually restore the old photograph itself. Instead, they make a copy of the original photo and then go to work with airbrushes on the copy. The original is returned to you in the same condition as when you sent it in.

The best part about their service is the price; it's quite reasonable, so you can add a nice markup and still make good money without overcharging your client. However, each piece they do is an original. So if you order more than one, there's no reduction in price for second and third copies.

Although the prices are good and the work is excellent, you'll have to allow some time to get your order back. Companies that do this type of work usually have brochures, price lists, and order materials.

Copy Work for Artists

Copying a piece of art is just like copying a photograph. I have several accounts with artists. Often they need color slides of their paintings to submit as entries to competitions in lieu of the actual paintings. Some artists also use slides for their files; others use them for reproduction in magazines, brochures, or other publications.

I always do this type of copy work outside, because I find I don't have to worry about color balance or changing the colors in the paintings when I use daylight Kodachrome and sunlight, or Ektachrome and sunlight.

Again, I use my kindergarten easel for this type of work. Some of the paintings are framed, some unframed. But they're both easy to prop up on the easel, because the easel has a little metal tray on the bottom to hold bottles of poster paint, and the paintings can sit on this.

I've also been called on by museums to make slides of some of their paintings and artifacts. On valuable pieces like these, I do all the work on location, but I still prefer to take the art outside to photograph, if it's possible to move it.

You might check with any local museums, or even historical societies, to see if they have any work for you along these lines. Some may even have old negatives or glass plates they would like to have prints made from.

Many freelancers shy away from copy work because they think it's difficult and time-consuming. I've always found it to be just the opposite. Most of the time it's something that you can work into your schedule when it's convenient for you. If you let it be known that you specialize in copy work, chances are you'll soon find that it's an important part of your income.

Chapter Twenty-seven

Assignments from Established Studios

(Work for a competitor? Yes!)

Ask an established studio photographer what he thinks about freelance photographers, and his answer usually won't be very complimentary. It'll probably come out something like this:

"Those blankety-blank moonlighters. They claim they don't have any overhead and can afford to work cheaper than I can. They practically give their pictures away. Seems like every third person you meet on the street has a camera hung around his neck and calls himself a photographer. 'What f-stop you using?' That's all they know how to say. I wish somebody would pass a law that said they had to take an exam before they could call themselves photographers. I have people coming into my studio all the time wanting me to *fix up* photos that freelancers have messed up."

Unfortunately, what the studio photographer says and thinks about freelancers is true in far too many cases. Don't fall into the category he's describing.

Don't give your work away. Don't try to make money on photography at another photographer's expense by offering to do for $15 what you know is at least a $100 job.

And don't ever ask another photographer what f-stop he's using! What good is that information going to do you, anyway. You don't know what kind of film he has loaded, what type of effect he's shooting for, how powerful his strobe is, or how much he's going to "push" the film in developing. Why do you want to know his f-stop? Calculate your own, taking *your* factors into consideration. When people start asking *you* "what's your f-stop," you'll know how annoying it is and how stupid it makes you sound.

Studio Photographers Need You

Studio photographers look down their noses at freelancers—except when they have to say no to a big client because everyone on their staff is already out on an assignment. Then, you can bet your boots that if the studio photographer knows a *good* freelancer, he'll call on that person for help.

If you're called in on such a job, and if you decide to accept the assignment, take extra time to make certain you know exactly what it entails. Get the studio photographer to give you the assignment in writing, detailing all the specifics, down to the type of film he wants you to use, the lighting, the placement of subjects—everything.

Often, when studio owners pass out photographic assignments to their own staffers, they don't take the time to go into specifics, because the staffers already know how the owners want things done. In dealing with you as a freelancer, an owner may assume that you know things that only his staffers would know.

Tell him why you're asking him all these questions. You need to know *exactly how he wants it done* if you're to give him the kind of results he wants.

Get to Know Them. All photographers like to talk shop. If there are studios in your town, make it a point to drop by and introduce yourself. Don't take up an owner's time if he's obviously busy. Just tell him you'd like to get together sometime for a cup of coffee or lunch.

If there's a commercial photography or communications group where you live, be sure to join. Attending meetings and socials is a great way to pick up some tips and get to know the other professional photographers in your area. Once you get to know a studio photographer, tell him that if he ever gets in a bind as far as assignments go, you'll be glad to help him out.

Once your reputation is established, studio photographers will probably come looking for you. That's the way it was in my case. Usually I was asked to help out by shooting weddings and aerial photographs. I once got a call on Saturday afternoon from an anxious photographer. He had become involved in a wreck while he was on the way to shoot a wedding. I was able to rush to the church and do the wedding for him. Needless to say, I made a good friend as well as a good business contact by being able to pull him out of that rough spot.

Studios that shoot a lot of proms often find they have two scheduled at the same time, or one oversized one that requires the services of more photographers than they have available on staff. I've heard of dances so large they kept four or five photographers busy shooting the whole night.

Let a studio owner know you're available, and the next time he has
more jobs than he can handle at once, he'll probably call on you to
lend a hand. It's a good way to pick up extra bucks—whether he wants
you to photograph a Mr. and Mrs. or a missile.

How to Charge

In a situation where you're asked to work on a job like a large prom, the studio photographer will probably offer you a flat fee for your help. When you're asked to handle a job completely for him, the fair way is to figure how much you'd have made if *you* had gotten the job in the first place. If the studio owner wants to furnish the materials, subtract their cost from the figure. Be sure to include travel expenses. You're doing the work; so you should be the one to make the money on the job. You're doing the studio owner a favor. If he wants to charge the customer a surcharge on top of your charges, that's up to him. Naturally, he'll also handle the processing and delivery of the order.

When you do a job of this type, never go back to the customer and try to get more of his business for yourself. But if the customer is so impressed with you and your work that *he* calls *you,* that's different!

When you're called on to work for a studio owner, then you're a *subcontractor,* and you know what good money those people make! But don't take advantage of the situation and try to stick it to the studio owner—not if you want more work or want to be able to call on him when you get in trouble. Never pop a flash in a man's eyes when you've got him pinned!

Job Offer?

If you start receiving calls from a studio owner to help out with his work load on a regular basis, don't be surprised if he offers you a full-time job. In some parts of the country, there seems to be a pretty high turnover rate among studio staff photographers. Many studios find they have trouble keeping young photographers, many of whom have been lured to the field by the excitement and glamour, only to find out that a great deal of studio work is rather routine or repetitive.

You'll have to make the decision whether you want to be tied in with a studio or to keep the greater freedom your freelance work offers.

Chapter Twenty-eight

Miscellaneous Money- Makers and Other Helpful Tips

(How many more can you think of?)

There's no way I can tell you everything you want or need to know about being a freelance photographer. I've attempted to organize this book in some logical sequence to provide the information that I've found to be important to me in my career. Here are some bits and pieces, ideas that didn't need a chapter, but could be useful to you. Miscellaneous is truly the word for this collection.

Airport Business

Remember the chapter on marinas? You can bet that airplane owners are as proud of their airplanes as boat owners are of their boats. Talk with the local flight service operator about letting you set up a weekend session to photograph people with their airplanes. Offer prom sets or 8x10s.

In most states airplane owners have what they call a breakfast club. All club members will fly somewhere once or twice a month for a breakfast meeting. They move these meetings around all over the state. If they ever come into your area, this would be an ideal time to offer such photographs. Some of these clubs have eighty or more planes fly in for each meeting.

You've probably heard advertisements about a local flying club's cooperating with a charitable organization in offering plane rides over the city or surrounding countryside in exchange for a donation. You could probably work something out with the sponsoring charity so that, for an additional contribution, you could photograph the people getting into the airplane. Part of that money would go to you and part to the charity.

Antique Dealers and Auctioneers

Many of the larger antique dealers print up brochures on special or unusual pieces and mail them out all across the country. Some also use color slides to send to other dealers or out-of-town customers.

Auctioneers sometimes print brochures, or even booklets, when they're called on to handle a valuable estate, a bankruptcy sale of a large business or industry, or some other large job. They also use color slides for TV ads or club presentations to help promote their sales.

I was hired once to produce a brochure for an auction sale of a large estate. The job continued to grow until it ended up as a sixteen-page tabloid chock full of photographs and descriptions of the items.

Apartment Buildings and Condos

Every time a new apartment complex or condo is completed, or an old one redecorated, the owners need photographs of model units to help lease or sell apartments. Check with the managers, and make sure they know your services are available.

The same is true with office complexes and industrial parks. Call on all of them.

Arts and Crafts

Many stores that sell supplies in this field also conduct classes in the various arts and crafts. Many of them, and their customers or students, take part in arts and crafts fairs or shows, where they sell their creations.

Some use photographs and color slides quite extensively, both for selling purposes and for keeping records of pieces they've sold.

Dermatologists

I've had good working relationships with several dermatologists in my area. Most of them like "before and after" photographs of some of their patients—especially those selected for dermabrasion, a process to help people with acne or other complexion problems.

Some of these photos are made in the doctor's office, some in the patient's home, some at my place. They are usually paid for by the patient. Be sure to give the patient a receipt; such photographs are a tax-deductible expense for him.

Usually three poses are required: left profile, right profile, and full face. If the person has long hair, pull the hair back behind the ears. Ears should always be shown. These photos are not designed to flatter the subject. They should be a true presentation of the subject's condition, and are strictly for-the-record photographs.

A Fair Booth

I've known some photographers who made it a point always to have a booth at the county or state fair. They would do uncomplicated work like making photo identification cards, especially for young children. A good selling point was that youngsters might get lost at the fair and the identification cards could be used by fair officials to contact their parents.

If you have a Polaroid camera like the one we discussed in Chapter 25, on passport and application photography, then you're all set for your own fair booth. In addition to the identification cards, you could offer mini-portraits in both black-and-white and color.

I don't believe I've ever talked to anyone who lost money with a fair booth of any kind. Fairgoers are a great bunch of clients.

Golf Courses

In addition to checking with the pro at your local golf course or country club about a new color photograph to be used on the scorecard, mention to him the possibility of allowing you to offer action photos to the golfers.

When the club is having a local tournament (or on any busy weekend), set up your camera on the first tee. Get a group shot of the foursome; then take an action photo of each golfer as he or she swings. With an assistant and a stabilization processor, you could have photos ready by the time they finish the round. Your assistant would pick up the film from you and process it, while you stay on the tee, shooting each group.

Display the photos in the clubhouse, and let the golfers purchase them right on the spot. Be sure you have enough prints of the group shots. If one member of a foursome buys a print, you can bet the rest of them probably will also.

Health Spas and Clubs

Many health clubs also suggest "before and after" photos for their members, usually paid for by the members although some clubs include this service in their overall membership fees. You won't need to take a lot of trouble in shooting the before photograph. In the after shot, make certain that the subject's hair has been done and the clothing is nice but not gaudy. You want to show the great results that have been achieved.

Just about everything you happen across can be a miscellaneous money-maker. Try your hand at photographing "scenics" on speculation; many businesses use them for decoration. The silhouette effect above is a different treatment of a beautiful work of art. The statue on page 185 is only a couple of feet high, but from a low camera angle it appears to be giant size—in front of a castle wall (the wall is only about four feet high).

In most cases the subject is standing flat-footed and slightly hunched in the before shot, and in an erect stance with feet in the "modeling" position in the after shot.

These organizations also use a lot of photos of their facilities for brochures, for portfolios for membership salespeople, and for display purposes.

It's worth a visit to try to line one up as a client, but be prepared for a sales pitch yourself. They'll try to sell you a membership! And believe me, they're good at it, too; you might learn a thing or two about selling.

Hospitals

Most hospitals, especially those in small towns, are nonprofit organizations. They're forever carrying on fund-raising projects of one kind or another, and often need photographs for brochures and booklets to help bring in the money.

Hospitals also have newsletters that use photos, as well as brochures for patients. You'll run into some hospitals that need slide presentations or other training aids for the staff.

I've known of some hospitals that had working agreements with freelance photographers to come in every morning and photograph newborn infants in the nursery. Parents usually have to shoot these photos through the glass, but the photographer was allowed inside the nursery with appropriate gown and mask. These photos were then offered to the parents. Naturally, additional copies were available to send to proud grandparents.

You can check with your hospital's public relations department or with the administrator's office for hospital photo possibilities.

Piano and Organ Teachers

Almost all piano and organ teachers schedule recitals once (maybe even twice!) a year. Prom sets, just like the ones you sell in dance schools, can be very popular almong musicians who are all dressed up and ready to perform.

It's best to pose students at the instrument after the recital. They're too nervous to photograph before, and you certainly don't want to take the chance of interrupting them with a flash while they're performing.

I photographed my first recital when my own children were taking piano lessons. I was only going to do this to get photos of my own, but quite a few of the other parents wanted their children photographed too. After this accidental discovery of a new source of freelance business, I began actively soliciting accounts from other music teachers.

Rent a Pony

Did you ever hear about the old-time photographers who would travel from town to town and door to door with their ponies in tow? For a fee, youngsters could climb in the saddle and have their pictures taken. Your parents or grandparents will remember the pony photographers.

This is a good one for a school carnival or a shopping center promotion. All you have to do is rent a gentle pony, have an assistant standing by in case the animal or child gets a little skittish, and you're in business. (As we discussed earlier, you'll want to make certain you have plenty of liability insurance coverage just in case there's an accident.)

At a school carnival, you'll have to give the school a cut of the money, but you'll also have an eager audience. The old pony-picture routine will bring back memories to a lot of the older folks—and there are probably more parents and grandparents than children at a school carnival anyway!

Restaurants

In addition to selling restaurants color postcards or decorative display prints, also sell them on the idea of photos for their menu covers. You could photograph the chef with a beautiful food creation, the owner seating a couple at a luxuriously set table, a full house enjoying dining—the possibilities are endless.

Ski Clubs

Both water and snow ski clubs have various competitions, within each club and with other organizations. Some also have performance teams which give shows for various groups. Group photographs of the club or of competition teams and photos of individual performers are good possibilities. Your polarizing filter will again be a help to you in cutting down on reflections from water or snow.

You can find out about water-ski clubs by checking with marinas and boat dealers. For snow ski clubs, check with lodges and shops that sell ski equipment.

Teaching

Just about every type of educational institution around these days offers courses in photography at one time or another. Just recently I've heard of courses offered in larger high schools, technical schools, junior colleges, community colleges, and the community schools for adults sponsored by most school districts. Some of the larger camera stores have classes; so do some museums. Most of these courses are open

to the general public as well as students of the particular institution.

Someone has to teach all of these courses. Often the instructor is hired on a part-time basis just to handle that one particular offering. If you're inclined toward teaching, you might enjoy such an activity, while picking up some additional spending money. While you won't get rich, when figured on an hourly basis for the actual time involved, the pay is usually quite good.

If you're interested, check around with some of the institutions in your area, and let them know you're available. They'll want to know something of your background and see some of your work.

Most of these courses are very basic, although some institutions also offer advanced courses. The atmosphere in the classes is usually very casual and easygoing.

A Magazine—a Free One

In my opinion, one of the best magazines published for the working photographer is available *absolutely free* to you as a freelancer. *Studio Photography* is billed as "the timely magazine for the professional portrait and commercial photographer." Published monthly, it's available free to studios, independent or freelance photographers, and newspaper or magazine photographers.

It contains many timely articles on various aspects of the business, articles on how to handle different accounts, interviews with well-known studio owners and photographers in all the fields, personal experience stories, technical articles, and photo features. It also contains timely tips on new products, industry news, and book reviews. You'll find many lab services among its advertisements, as well as other services needed by freelance photographers.

To have your name added to the subscription list, write: *Studio Photography,* 250 Fulton Ave., Hempstead, NY 11550.

Ask them to send you a subscription application form. It's best to write to them on your business letterhead.

More Publications. Eastman Kodak Company has many publications for photographers; some are free and some you'll have to pay for. Write and ask for a list of available publications: Consumer Markets Division, Eastman Kodak Company, Rochester, NY 14650.

If you're having any technical problems in your darkroom work, it wouldn't hurt to drop them a line and explain what difficulties you're encountering. I've always found them very helpful.

Negative Files

Always maintain your negative files in good order. They can be a gold mine. You never know when somebody is going to want reprints of a job you did several years ago. Many times business and industry people will call on you looking for stock aerial photos of a certain intersection on the interstate highway or of an industrial park or shopping center. People who buy passport and application photos invariably need more copies than the amount they first order. I once sold a complete remake of a wedding album to a woman whose house burned five years after the wedding!

You never know when those negative files will turn out to be money in the bank.

A Final Word:

The Real Reward

One of the things I've always enjoyed about being a freelance photographer is that you have the chance to make so many people happy—to provide them with lasting memories of special occasions, which they'll cherish. By photographing their weddings, their children, their pets, their leisure-time activities, their business activities, and their special honors and awards, you become a part of people's happy times. Whether as a part-time activity to help bring in a second income or as a full-time vocation, what more rewarding career could one ask for than to be paid for doing something so worthwhile? Sure, making $25,000 a year from your photography is great, but there's more to any worthwhile vocation than just the money.

"Photographers are a *dime a dozen!*" How many times have you heard that expression? "What? You're going to become a photographer too? There's already one on every street corner." I'll never agree with that. *Picture takers are a dime a dozen. Real photographers are the rare exception!* When one comes along, it doesn't take people long to find out, and to start seeking his or her services.

Word-of-mouth advertising is the key. You can't buy it, no matter how much you're willing to pay. It's just like respect; it has to be earned, and it has to be deserved. My work speaks for me. What I produce for my clients establishes my reputation and my identity.

Clients know when they contract for my services that I won't attempt to run, or to ruin, their show. Whether I'm in their homes or at their places of business, I consider myself a guest—a paid guest, but a guest nonetheless. I attempt to dress and conduct myself as any other guest invited to the occasion, whatever it may be.

I've always taken pride in the fact that, while I believed I was one of the most important people at any event I recorded on film, I've also been able to stay in the background and be possibly the most inconspic-uous person there. I don't want to be known as "that pushy photogra-pher who orders everyone around." Sure, I tell people what I want and need to do my job. I pose them and put them in position so they'll look good. But giving direction and ordering are two different things.

There may be room in the profession for the temperamental, the self-centered, or the eccentric, but I've never needed to find that place. There's always room, and there always will be work, for the good photographer—the person who can do an honest job for an honest price.

My work will be around long after me. I take satisfaction in knowing that I've been, and will continue to be, a part of other people's good times and good memories.

Index